DIFFERENT

How the power of different and AI can amplify your brand

Varsha Amin

G₁P

Grosvenor House
Publishing Limited

This book is published by
Grosvenor House Publishing Ltd
Link House
140 The Broadway, Tolworth, Surrey, KT6 7HT.
www.grosvenorhousepublishing.co.uk

A CIP record for this book
is available from the British Library

Paperback ISBN 978-1-83615-198-2
eBook ISBN 978-1-83615-199-9

DEDICATION

To my beautiful girls, Arya and Ava, my greatest inspirations. You remind me every day of the strength found in love, curiosity, and resilience.

This book is a testament to the world I hope to help shape for you—a kinder, fairer, and more inclusive one.

And to my grandfather and father, whose wisdom, values, and unwavering belief in me have been my guiding lights. Your legacies are woven into every word of this book.

Thank you for teaching me the power of kindness and determination.

This is for you.

CONTENTS

WHY THESE WORDS MATTER

I'm writing this book to build a world where kindness and inclusivity are the norm, not the exception. I want to inspire you to be the change you wish to see in the world.

I've faced my fair share of challenges, but I've learned that adversity can be a catalyst for growth. It's about pushing beyond limits, daring to be different, and creating a ripple effect of positive change. Your personal brand is a powerful tool; use it wisely.

Remember, you have the power to shape your world. Your actions and values matter. Let's build a future where being different isn't just accepted but celebrated; a world where we embrace AI (Artificial Intelligence) to power and amplify our brands so that we're not only seen but heard.

By choosing this book, you're taking the first step on an extraordinary journey of impact.

Thank you for being part of this movement.

DARE TO BE DIFFERENT. EVERYONE ELSE IS TAKEN.

INTRODUCTION

'Be the change-maker that you were born to be'.

As I edit these words in August 2024, I'm filled with sadness watching the protests and the rise in hate crimes sweeping across the UK — fuelled by fake news and propaganda. This has to end, for the sake of our children and their future. As my awareness grows, I'm noticing the tension points more clearly. When I travelled from Winchester to London for work, the stark reality hit home: I was the only person of colour walking to the office in Marylebone, London. The streets were nearly empty, and the trains had only a handful of people of colour.

That same day, I got a notification that far-right groups were planning riots across the UK, one of which was set for Hounslow. I froze, fearing for my sister's wellbeing and that of my parents. I immediately grabbed my phone and sent the message: 'Don't go into the office. Stay at home.' The next day, I broke down in tears. How did we ever get here? This isn't the world I want for my children.

What troubled me most was realising that much of the fear and hype was fuelled by fake news. People were scared. I was scared. I couldn't help but wonder how much Generative AI (GenAI) had contributed to this frenzy.

The world is changing rapidly, both socially and technologically. GenAI is here, and we must adapt and innovate. Technology should be a force for good. But let's be real—many of us feel like we're barely holding on. The world of work, especially for those who are under-represented, has never been more challenging.

I'm here to show you how to level the playing field—how you can lift yourself and others up at the same time. The key? Your personal brand. I'll give you insights and strategies to help you build a strong personal brand, to help you amplify your brand, improve your visibility, and to be heard in a sector that is difficult to succeed in, particularly if you're under-represented.

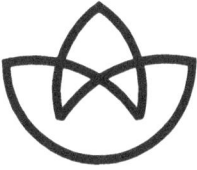

Be the change-maker that you were born to be.

___

VARSHA AMIN

What's wrong with the technology industry?

Tech is supposed to be at the frontier of innovation, yet it still clings to an outdated 'boys' club' mentality. This mindset marginalises those who don't fit the mould, hitting under-represented groups the hardest.

The struggles of working mothers

Women, especially working mothers in tech, face immense challenges. Balancing a demanding career with parental responsibilities is tough, and the high cost of childcare only adds to the burden. For many, leaving the workforce or accepting a demotion becomes a necessity rather than a choice, reinforcing gender inequality and depriving industries of diverse talent.

We need solutions:—flexible working hours, subsidised childcare, and initiatives that truly support working parents, especially mothers. It's time to stop forcing capable women to take a step back. Instead, let's empower them to step forward.

Ethnic minorities in tech

Professionals from ethnic minority backgrounds face their own set of obstacles in tech. Despite growing awareness about the need for inclusivity, unequal opportunities remain a harsh reality.

Authenticity is crucial for career growth, yet many fear that being true to themselves will hinder their advancement. This book offers strategies for building a personal brand that not only embraces your identity but also challenges stereotypes. I'll share my story and show you how to leverage your cultural heritage as a strength in the tech world.

The power of neurodiversity

Neurodiversity, which includes conditions like autism, attention deficit hyperactivity disorder (ADHD), and dyslexia, can bring unique strengths to the table: skills like computational thinking, pattern recognition, and adaptability. These are invaluable in tech, yet the industry struggles to integrate neurodiverse talent.

We need to raise awareness, adjust recruitment processes, and create inclusive workplaces that recognise and harness these strengths. Companies that want to attract neurodiverse talent should have neurodiverse leaders and teams driving these initiatives. If they don't, then we need to push for change.

My journey with dyslexia

As someone with dyslexia, I know the challenges it brings. But I also know the strengths that it offers: creative thinking, problem-solving, and seeing the bigger picture. Dyslexia isn't just a challenge; it can be an advantage.

This book isn't just about highlighting the struggles; it's about showing you how to turn your differences into strengths. Whether you're neurodiverse or not, I want to offer you a roadmap to success in the tech world.

Limited opportunities

I say this as a woman of colour who felt completely disconnected from the corporate world while raising my firstborn away from London. I looked for a part-time role locally, but nothing suitable was available. For the roles that companies in Hampshire did offer, I wasn't even given the opportunity for an interview. Was it my name, my ethnicity, or perhaps my tech background? I was certainly qualified for those positions. Or was it unconscious bias at play? It didn't take long for me to realise that I had much better prospects in London. That's when my focus shifted—from searching for opportunities in Winchester, to realising that London was where I truly belonged. After all, London is deeply woven into the fabric of my brand's identity and DNA. I'll explain what I mean by this later, but for now, stay with me...

This book is for everyone

This book is for anyone feeling marginalised or under-represented in tech—or any industry. I'm advocating for a world where diversity isn't just a checkbox, but a celebrated asset. Personal branding is a powerful tool in this fight, helping you stand out in a world that often overlooks the under-represented.

A call for change

This book is more than a guide; it's a call to action. I want to empower you to claim your space, to build a personal brand that challenges norms and drives change. Through personal stories, expert insights, and actionable strategies, I hope to inspire and equip you to thrive in a tech industry that's slowly waking up to the power of diversity and authenticity.

You are valuable, just as you are.

So, let's start this journey together.

PART ONE

WHAT NEEDS TO CHANGE

PART ONE: WHAT NEEDS TO CHANGE

There's a lot of work that needs to be done to make the changes I've mentioned, and the good news is that you can start with your personal brand. You don't need a huge following; you just need a handful of good people to advocate for you, if they're not doing so already. Before I go into this, let's understand what a personal brand is.

1. WHAT IS A PERSONAL BRAND?

A personal brand is the unique blend of your qualities, values and experiences that sets you apart. It's how you present yourself, what you stand for and how you make others feel. In today's world, *you* are a brand, whether you realise it or not.

Every interaction, every word, every action, contributes to how others perceive you. Your personal brand is your story, authentically told, and it holds the power to shape your career, your opportunities, and your impact. Let's add more definition to this by taking a look at explanations available to us of what a personal brand is.

To find out, I asked a generative AI tool which I have named Sai. Here's what it suggested:

> *'A personal brand is the authentic expression of your unique qualities and values, shaping how others perceive and connect with you.*

> *It's your story, consistently told through actions and words, that sets you apart and drives your impact.'*

I love that Sai could answer this based on how I have been training it.

But then I looked for an expert opinion to validate this:

I love this simple definition by Hannah Power[1]:

> *'Anyone who is actively making themselves known for something is a personal brand.'*

> *'Your brand is your message, your movement, and your tribe is waiting.'*

I agree with this, but I'd also add that it's how you make others feel, and the experience you deliver.

For me:

> *Brand is the sum of everything: what you stand for, what you say, what you do, how you do it—and how you make others feel.*

Brand is everything and everything is brand.

In my world everyone is a brand. This means you're a brand—a personal brand.

---

[1] Hannah Power, *The Power of You* (2019), p22.

You carry weight, you matter, and so does what you stand for—whether you're starting out with big aspirations, or you're an established leader within the tech industry.

Your value will be perceived based on what others believe you are worth. Personal branding isn't a new concept. I first encountered it at university in 2004. My interest in the subject led me to dedicate my entire dissertation to exploring the idea of brand. Fast-forward to today, and it's become a widely recognised phenomenon.

If you're currently not capitalising on the full potential of your personal brand, consider what you read next as a call to act:

- It might surprise you to learn that up to **95% of business clients** are not in the market for goods and services at any one time. According to the Ehrenberg-Bass Theory, 95% of potential buyers are not actively considering a purchase. This is called the 95-5 Rule, and it shows the importance of building strong brand awareness for all customers in the customer-buying journey, not just the active buyers in the 5% crowd. This means that amplifying your brand now will make it attract opportunities in the future.

- The importance of brand authenticity in today's market is further backed up by consumer research from Sprout Social[2], which found that **76% of consumers** would buy

---

[2] Accessed January 2025: https://sproutsocial.com/insights/data/social-media-connection/

from a brand they feel connected to over a competitor. This is why story telling with an emotional connection is such an important component of brand building.

- According to Google's 7-11-4 Rule, a prospective client needs to be engaged with content for about seven hours to build trust and connection and be converted. This engagement should take place across 11 touch points and in four different locations of contact. This means continuously being present where it matters the most.

- According to a research study by Profile[3], nearly **70% of respondents** said that they trust companies with visible leaders more than those without. This is because consumers are increasingly interested in learning about the people behind the brands they like.

So, you'll understand why amplifying your brand now will make it attract the opportunities in the future. I have seen this happen for me; it can happen for you.

You already know how essential personal branding is for maximising your earning power in the current economy we live in, since you're reading this book.

---

[3] Accessed January 2025: https://welcometoprofile.com/insight/2023/01/19/research-thought-leadership-boosts-a-company-s-bottom-line

Take a look at the Google Trends graph below. Over the past 20 years, interest in personal branding has steadily climbed, proving this isn't just a passing trend—it's the future:

The world is slowly waking up and realising the incredible opportunities that come with having a strong personal brand. For example, attracting employers and clients towards you without you chasing them, or being picked among dozens of candidates for the job you applied for just because your LinkedIn profile stood out (this has happened to me).

Why am I telling you this?

In the age of GenAI, you're really going to struggle to stand out, unless you get ahead of the curve, like pronto! Now is the time to invest in your personal brand. If you've already started, great work.

Personal branding is now a multimillion-dollar industry. Think of companies that brand celebrities—they make millions, so do celebrities. But this book isn't about them; this book is about how a person from an under-represented, different background, can use the power of their brand to be heard. We're in 2025, and yet we still haven't caught onto the power of brand, so this is your chance to take the first step, to make an impact. That window is still open, but it will change and evolve as more of us leverage GenAI.

But what is GenAI, and what does it mean for brand, given that the adoption rate of GenAI is growing exponentially? Let's find out.

What is Generative AI?

GenAI is a type of artificial intelligence that can create new content—whether it's text, images, music, or even code—by learning from existing data. Instead of simply following preset instructions, GenAI analyses patterns and generates unique outputs based on what it has learned. Think of it as a powerful tool that amplifies creativity and innovation, helps you to produce content that represents your brand with speed and scale, aiding you to amplify your personal brand in ways that were previously not possible.

They say that your brand isn't what you say it is, it's what others say it is. Well, that at least is the phrase you hear banded about.

However, for 2025 and beyond, the reality now is that your brand isn't what you say it is; it's what GenAI says it is.

Just think about it. I Googled myself recently, and I came across the following:

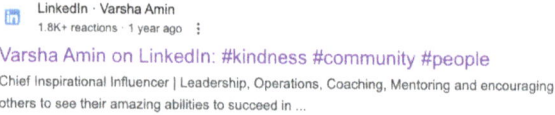

in LinkedIn · Varsha Amin
1.8K+ reactions · 1 year ago ⋮

Varsha Amin on LinkedIn: #kindness #community #people
Chief Inspirational Influencer | Leadership, Operations, Coaching, Mentoring and encouraging others to see their amazing abilities to succeed in ...

'Chief Inspirational Influencer'—I mean, I'll totally take that, thank you. Where it comes from, in truth, I'll never know. But my guess is that it's been organised by AI from a series of comments that I have responded to from a LinkedIn post that went viral.

I then typed the following into the search bar: **Who is Varsha Amin?**

This is the response I got back from Gemini AI, with of course a disclaimer: Generative AI is experimental.

> *'Varsha Amin is a brand strategist who helps entrepreneurs increase their visibility. She specialises in AI-powered branding, brand marketing, and global brand strategy. Amin is also a Gen-Z mentor. Amin believes that kindness is the best strategy in life, at work and in business. She has a community where people can be heard, seen and have a voice.'*

While this is a reasonable reflection of who I am, it doesn't include all my achievements and accolades, so in truth the AI is doing a disservice on exactly how valuable I am as a personal brand. This is why under-represented individuals and those that consider themselves marginalised have to step up their efforts to be seen and heard. With the power of AI, you can change it. So, embrace it now and allow it to amplify and accelerate your brand-building efforts.

Now try it for your personal brand and see what comes up. You'll be surprised at what you might find. If you don't come up, then this book will help you get started.

In my personal experience of social media platforms where I am seen and heard, my favoured one has to be LinkedIn. The algorithms allow my organic content to get the visibility it deserves. With Meta (Instagram, Facebook and Threads), I have personally found that if you are a new kid on the block trying to build your brand, the algorithms tend to suppress your organic brand reach and visibility. This is why I switched my focus entirely to LinkedIn, which effectively does the brand building for me and attracts a steady flow of opportunities.

Anyhow, let's continue from where we left off.

Remember, no matter who you are, or where you come from:

YOU ARE WORTHY. YOU DEFINE YOUR OWN WORTH.

Let's explore this further and make it meaningful to you.

2. YOU HAVE A POWERFUL BRAND

'Your brand is the sum of everything'.

Your brand is the sum of everything—how you act, your values, what you say, what you do, and why you do it. It tells your story and makes you visible. This isn't just a mindset shift; it's a life-changing tool. I'm not just a mother, wife, daughter, employee, or businesswoman—I'm a brand. And so are you. Embrace this thinking, and your brand will change your life and career, as it has mine.

The power of your personal brand

As Simon Sinek famously stated, 'People don't buy what you do; they buy why you do it.' Your brand is the embodiment of that 'why'. Let it do the heavy lifting for you, consistently showcasing your values and actions. As Jeff Bezos once said, 'Your brand is what people say about you when you're not in the room.'

I believe everyone is a brand. This isn't just a buzzword; it's a powerful reality. I'd go as far as to say **your personal brand is your most valuable asset.** But how can you use your brand to level the playing field if you're under-represented?

Personal branding is vital, especially for those marginalised by factors such as ethnicity, gender, or neurodiversity. A strong brand offers visibility, recognition, and better opportunities for career advancement.

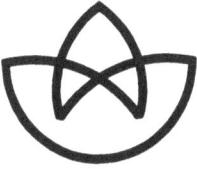

Your brand is the sum of everything.

VARSHA AMIN

Workplace bias is real. A 2019 survey by The Guardian[4] found that 57% of people from ethnic minorities felt they had to overperform to stay on par with their peers, driven by the pressure to break stereotypes. This overperformance isn't a choice—it's a necessity. The same survey revealed that 43% believed that they were unfairly denied promotions due to their ethnicity, highlighting systemic barriers in the workplace.

But there's also empowerment. A strong brand helps minority leaders overcome bias and thrive.

---

[4] Accessed January 2024: https://www.theguardian.com/world/2019/jan/17/minority-ethnic-britons-face-shocking-job-discrimination

Your personal brand is more than an image or persona; it's the embodiment of your authentic self. It's about using your identity, experiences and perspectives to create a unique profile. For under-represented groups, this can be transformative, providing a platform to challenge the status quo and amplify their voices, often unheard in corporate cultures.

Building your personal brand

Building your personal brand starts with understanding and accepting your authentic self. This involves introspection to identify your core values, strengths and unique perspectives. For people from ethnic minorities, it may also mean embracing aspects of identity and culture previously downplayed in professional settings.

The power of story telling

Story telling is a powerful element of branding. It builds muscle memory and raises your profile by highlighting your unique journey; the obstacles you've overcome, and the perspective you bring to your field. Your narrative is a compelling tool to connect with others, inspire empathy, and dismantle preconceived notions.

The bigger picture

The tech industry, for all its advancements, still has a long way to go on inclusivity and diversity. Apart from arming you with strategies to become visible, valuable, and attract the opportunities you deserve, I advocate for a kinder and more inclusive tech environment. Diversity should be celebrated, not just tolerated.

How does this relate to me, and how did I even get into this position?

Let me tell you my story.

3. MY STORY AND MY BRAND DNA

'From nothing to something'—it seems like such a cliché. But in this case, it truly and authentically encapsulates the essence of personal evolution, the bedrock of what I passionately term 'Brand DNA'.

A flight from Uganda

Before my story even began, its prologue was written on a plane fleeing Uganda. In 1972, my grandfather made the leap of a lifetime, escaping to the UK amidst the anti-Asian rage stoked by Uganda's then president Idi Amin. This harrowing beginning ironically became the foundation of our family's future, turning a journey of despair into one of possibilities.

When my grandfather defied fate, he didn't just survive—he rewrote the script of our family's DNA from scarcity to potential. This legacy of resilience taught me to turn stumbling blocks into stepping stones, forming the essence of who I have become today.

The spirit of transformation

This spirit of transformation isn't just my story; it's a philosophy that I want to pass on to you. Your Brand DNA isn't fixed—it's a living fabric, woven from your struggles, dreams, and growth. Every challenge that you overcome adds a new thread, making your DNA more powerful and uniquely yours.

Finding roots amidst struggle

Life in the UK was anything but easy. My family arrived with nothing but a single £50 note and hope, finding refuge in camps before finally putting down roots. Born in Hounslow, West London, I faced my own challenges early on—a heart defect that required major surgery at just three years old. That ordeal didn't just heal my physical heart; it fortified my emotional core, embedding resilience into my very being.

The emotional battleground

My childhood was an emotional battleground. My mother— loving yet strict—set impossibly high standards. Her love felt like chains at times, leaving me questioning my worth. My mother had high expectations of me, since she didn't have the time to do everything. I embraced a leadership role, caring for my three younger sisters and supporting my mother with house chores from the tender age of seven. I had to grow up fast. Those experiences later fuelled my vision of a world where 'being enough' isn't the exception but the norm. This emotional terrain became another strand in my Brand DNA—anchoring it in resilience and a relentless pursuit of transformation.

'Dedi' and the hurdles

My father—my 'dedi'—was my anchor in life's storms. His unwavering belief in me transformed struggles into launchpads. His faith taught me perseverance and the courage to defy societal norms. Through him, I discovered who I was, shaping a brand born from the test of personal challenges.

Rewriting the script

Being part of an under-represented group isn't just a label, it's a vantage point; a superpower embedded in my DNA. When I don't see people like me represented, I'm driven to break the mould. This determination, inspired by my family's journey from Uganda, taught me that negative thinking leads nowhere.

The '90s, with its flux of changing norms, could make one feel isolated for not fitting in. But here's the thing: I've never been one for mediocrity. My refusal to conform became a badge of honour, a defining feature that enriched my brand and my vision of a world that finds beauty in imperfections. As it became a part of me, it became a part of the future self I'd want to signpost and show off to the world.

Parts of me were fundamentally growing through this time. I was a passionate writer of fiction then, and my venture into the realm of storytelling was met with accolades, even when my English teacher cast doubts. It solidified my belief in a world where academic laurels don't dictate your worth—it's you who dictates your worth. It wasn't just writing, though; I expressed myself through dance. Dance, for me, became more than a hobby. It was an alternative voice, one that graced school stages and spoke volumes. This artistic avenue added a dimension to my burgeoning personal brand, affirming in me the need for multifaceted talents in a world that should celebrate 'being enough' as the norm.

My dyslexic mind: a revelation

College was a mix of emotions. I floundered after failing my A-Levels, lost and confused until, at 20, I was diagnosed with dyslexia. It was like finding the missing piece of a puzzle. Suddenly, my academic struggles made sense, and I could finally tailor my learning and thrive with the support that I deserved.

This diagnosis was a turning point, reinforcing my belief that challenging the status quo isn't rebellion—it's a mark of integrity. It sparked a dream: a world where your academic transcript doesn't define your worth; a world guided by humanity, not algorithms.

Daring to defy

Post-university, while searching for jobs I found myself awash in rejection letters. So, I threw out the rule book, ditching the norms of CV crafting. Out went the conventional templates; in came audacious creativity—coloured paper, unconventional layouts, and a cheeky tone. This maverick approach landed me a role at a travel and lifestyle super brand in London, catapulting me into a realm of professional growth that later saw me collaborate with leading tech giants like Apple. But this wasn't merely a job switch; it was a validation of my inherent belief in challenging established norms.

The corporate labyrinth

The trajectory of my career shot up—big tech giants, accolades aplenty. But let me be honest with you, it wasn't a walk in the park. These zigzags in my professional journey were essential milestones in moulding my personal brand. They taught me another invaluable lesson: that life's zeniths are littered with troughs, and that it's our resilience in navigating these that truly defines us.

Are you starting to see a theme in my personal brand and its evolution? Could it be about overcoming adversity and being relentless in your pursuit of what you think you deserve? If so, you'd be right. But there's another aspect to this: no excuses. This is what made *me*, but life is what I've made *it*.

The 2000s continued to temper my personal brand into its current form. They instilled in me the virtues of resilience and the audacity to question societal norms. More importantly, they made me realise that my personal brand wasn't just an extension of me; it was a reflection of the change I wish to see in this world. And it was during this period that I began mentoring the next generation, sharing nuggets of wisdom gleaned from my own journey, thereby extending the reach of my personal brand.

So, you can see the synergy between my personal brand, the story of how it came to form, and how this relates to you as a reader. Because that relationship is fundamental to everything I, and by extension you, want to achieve, as well as the wider impact these positive changes could have.

The grand corporate illusion

As I continued my journey through life, I began to climb the corporate ladder. I felt an unsettling shift within my core. The siren-call of high salaries and prestigious titles created a mirage, blurring my vision. The gilded cage I was in began to tarnish. The very success I had yearned for was eroding the foundations of my personal brand—my creativity, my wellbeing, and my individuality. In short, the very things that make me who I am.

When the soul pays the price

We all have our price, but have you ever stopped to think what yours is? As I navigated the complex maze of toxic work environments, the toll became painfully evident. I was trading my soul for a more impressive bank balance. Each passing day led me to ponder on the dissonance between societal markers of success and genuine human fulfilment. Could I find a middle ground? That existential question pushed me to revisit some of the values upon which I'd built my brand: kindness, innovation and, above all, human dignity.

The wake-up call that changed it all

The relentless pursuit of what society deemed 'successful' led to sleepless nights that turned into sleepless years. Finally, in 2015, it had developed from simply a rut or a low point to a deafening wake-up call; a call to realign my personal brand with my core values, values that had somehow got lost in the hustle. Was the pain of realignment excruciating? Absolutely. But it shored up my belief in a world that respects those who rise from the ashes, even if that rise culminates in a fall that serves as a stepping stone to something unimaginably greater.

4. THE IMPACT OF MOTHERHOOD

It was around this time that the magic of motherhood entered my life. It was a breath of the freshest air, a stark contrast to the stale and stifling atmosphere of office politics I had become accustomed to. But as I contemplated stepping back into my heels and rejoining the rat race, the old demons resurfaced: rigid work hours, toxic corporate cultures, and an alarming lack of local opportunities. It was as if the universe was testing me, nudging my self-worth to the brink. A cloud of despair began to form. In the labyrinth of my own thoughts and insecurities, I found myself wrestling with darker forces: crippling body-image issues, a plummeting sense of self-worth, and even thoughts so dark they whispered, 'Is life even worth it?' It was a tempest raging within the confines of my mind, threatening to annihilate my very essence, my brand, my identity.

But you know what they say: every crisis is an opportunity. It marked a beginning, a period of introspection and recalibration that forced me to rediscover what I stood for. And believe it or not, the corporate grind—both its peaks and its troughs—had the power to enrich my brand narrative. It added layers of complexity, making it relatable and, dare I say it, more authentic.

Before I continue my story, let's take a moment to reflect on some facts on the impact motherhood can have on a woman's career. The picture for pregnant women and mothers is quite bleak. A recent study by Pregnant Then

Screwed[5] has lifted the lid on workplace discrimination they currently face. The research reveals a pretty alarming trend: 52% of mothers have encountered some form of discrimination during pregnancy, maternity leave, or upon their return to work. This is awful to read, but not particularly shocking to mothers out there, I'm sure.

The study, prepared by IFF Research[6] on behalf of The Equality and Human Rights Commission and the Department for Business, Innovation and Skills, conducted in collaboration with Women In Data, surveyed over 24,000 parents. It brings to light not only the numerical extent of the issue, but also the cultural attitudes prevalent in workplaces today. The data indicates that one in five mothers (20%) have felt compelled to leave their jobs following adverse or discriminatory experiences. Additionally, 10% of women reported being bullied or harassed when pregnant or returning to work, and 7% of women lost their job—through redundancy, sacking, or feeling pressured to resign due to declined flexible working requests or health and safety concerns. This suggests that up to 41,752 pregnant women or mothers could be sacked or made redundant each year. Utterly awful, I'm sure you'll agree.

With that context in mind, let's continue with my story...

---

[5] Accessed January 2024: https://pregnantthenscrewed.com/about-maternity-discrimination/

[6] Pregnancy and Maternity–Related Discrimination and Disadvantage: Experiences of Mothers. Accessed October 2024: https://doc.ukdataservice.ac.uk/doc/7962/mrdoc/pdf/pregnancy-and-maternity-related-discrimination-and-disadvantage-experiences-of-mothers.pdf

The parental load and my mental health

After taking a career break, I faced an unrecognisable world. Now not just Varsha, but a mother to Arya, I felt like a foreigner in my own life. Corporate culture remained stubbornly insensitive to the needs of working parents. Each day turned into a battle for meaning, for relevance, for survival. But then, just when all seemed lost, a flicker of hope appeared. Realisation dawned that the only person who could pull me out of this abyss was me, aided by a few who still saw in me the brilliance that I had forgotten. Piece by piece, I began rebuilding my fractured soul, my brand, and my vision for a better world.

Here are just some of the things that I had to contend with:

- **Navigating life as a new mother.** I felt like a single parent, while my husband did his first consultant role and completed his PhD every weekend.

- **Feeling alone and isolated** and cut off from the world I knew. Nobody asked me if I was ok. I didn't even ask myself.

- **The darkness that engulfed me.** I could see myself in a black hole. Was I heading for depression?

I had no idea how to get myself out without a rope or anyone on the other side to lift me out. There was no light. Had I plunged myself into darkness and out of existence? I questioned my reasons for existing. All the confidence and the career and self-worth I had built over a decade felt eroded in the space of 12 months.

That was back in 2016, and now I can see that I really needed the help that did not exist and which I still struggle to find now. This is why I'm a big fan of the Mother Lovers – Let's Lighten the Load for Working Mums campaign by Maltesers[7] because it captures a key insight that more parents need support.

Being a parent, especially a working mum, is one of the toughest balancing acts imaginable. The constant juggling of work, home life, and personal responsibilities can feel overwhelming, leaving women exhausted and struggling to meet the expectations society places on them. This is where initiatives like the Real Out of Office movement by Maltesers come in, sparking much-needed conversations around the realities working mums face every day.

For parents in tech, especially those who feel marginalised, these challenges can be even more pronounced. My book's focus on helping under-represented groups build their personal brands ties into this movement beautifully. Just as the Real Out of Office movement encourages honesty about the struggles that mothers face, my book emphasises embracing our unique circumstances—whether that's parenting, cultural identity, or professional background—as strengths.

---

[7] Accessed October 2024: https://www.maltesers.co.uk/lighten-the-load

By the time 2018 rolled around, it was glaringly obvious that something had to give. The relentless years of corporate hustle and internal warfare had eroded the essence of my personal brand. And no amount of refreshing time away could change the damage that had been done. Was it time for a radical reset? Absolutely. I had to overhaul my internal operating system, delve deep into my core values, and breathe new life into the brand that was me.

The DNA of my brand was multifaceted by this point, punctuated by some key ideas, not least among them kindness, innovation, and technology. They weren't merely words on paper; they were a part of the foundational pillars of my identity. This wasn't just about picking up where I left off; it was about evolving. You see, I didn't discard the hard-earned lessons from my corporate years. Instead, I funnelled them into a more nuanced, more powerful vision, a vision in tune with a world I dreamed of, one built on the cornerstones of respect, empowerment, and human dignity.

This change in mindset had given birth to LotusX, my freelance training and coaching business, which would later become an anchor and stepping stone for newer opportunities, including those that I hadn't even considered before.

Entrepreneurship: a statement

Taking the entrepreneurial plunge wasn't merely a career pivot, it was a bold proclamation of my brand's ethos; a commitment not only to live my truth, but to inspire others to live theirs. This journey wasn't just about me; it was about catalysing a ripple effect in the wider world. Imagine a planet inhabited by fearless trailblazers who defy the conventional. Exciting, isn't it? And I couldn't expect others to blaze the trail for me. I had to make that move myself and hopefully inspire others to follow.

Not only did I carve a niche of professional success, but I also found myself again—my *essence*. This was no selfish triumph, it was a victory for the world I aspired to inhabit; a world that cherishes the 'oddballs', the 'underdogs' and the brave souls willing to challenge the status quo. This fresh chapter invigorated my brand, anchoring it firmly in its mission to ignite change. After all, where does transformation begin but deep within ourselves? If we can't believe in our own self-improvement and authenticity, how can we believe in anyone else?

The pandemic pivot

Ah, 2020, the year the world stood still, and my brand wobbled on its axis. Initially, my self-worth took a nosedive. Businesses shuttered, opportunities vanished, and it felt as though I was spiralling backwards, unravelling years of hard-won progress. Could my brand, founded on resilience and adaptability, weather this storm? The entire world was, to some extent or another, asking this question. It was an unprecedented time.

Then something extraordinary unfolded. As the world went virtual, I found myself living a dual life—all within the four walls of my home. Juggling professional commitments with maternal duties was a Herculean task, yet incredibly enlightening. It was a tough time for myself and my family, and I recall crying so much during that time, trying to juggle a job I loved with the pressures and turmoil that came with being in lockdown. It was breaking point for many working parents.

In the long run it granted me, as a working parent, a new way of working. Our homes became offices, and technology and systems became allies to enable hybrid working.

What was next for my brand?

As much as the pandemic added nuance to my personal brand, it also unveiled systemic flaws that I couldn't ignore—gender roles, mental health support, you name it. Aren't these societal issues my brand should confront head-on? Absolutely. The road ahead was clear: my brand, like me, was a perpetual work in progress.

In the midst of all this, I had an epiphany—my life's old programming was archaic, utterly incompatible with who I'd become and who I aspired to be. It was time for a software update. This new version had to be rooted in my brand's core DNA: kindness, challenging the status quo, and technology. But let's not forget, it had to begin with self-love because fundamentally I was, literally and metaphorically, hiding from myself.

There were some obvious examples. With not a single photo of me on social media, wasn't it obvious that I was spiralling into a vortex of self-neglect, yearning for external validation? The cycle had to be broken.

I used various methods to get through this time, methods that you may find useful on your own journey of self-discovery.

5. HOW I REPROGRAMMED MY MIND

'Transformation requires a reboot to the mindset'.

To help me find myself, my confidence, and worthiness, I started to think of my mind as a software program that needed upgrading, and I worked on rebuilding myself.

Installing 'new software' included doing the following four things:

1. **Gratitude meditation.** Each morning began with a ritual of counting my blessings, shifting from a static to a growth mindset.

2. **Building confidence.** I enlisted professionals to guide me through diverse life aspects: a confidence coach, a stylist for sartorial expression, and even a photographer to visually capture the 'new me'.

3. **Career reshaping.** Brand Strategist became my new title, merging my digital and tech passions to assist others.

4. **Continuous learning.** The odyssey towards my 'true self' was dotted with ceaseless growth, constant remastering, and iterative processes.

Transformation requires a reboot to the mindset.

———
VARSHA AMIN

Facing the mindset obstacle

But hold on, the journey wasn't all glorious. I still grappled with gnawing self-doubt and limiting beliefs. I had a coach at the time who helped me to focus my goals and to find where my problems lay. And they were right, there were mental barricades. My self-doubt needed to be checked by the evidence around me of positivity, and my clients' glowing testimonials added that extra layer of assurance.

I was undeniably on the right track. And those commendations rolled in like a flood—higher visibility on Google, soaring engagement rates, and audacious content strategies that defied norms. Wasn't this tangible proof that I was sitting atop a treasure trove of untapped potential? Absolutely, it was. And I was only able to perceive this by taking the risk of trusting my inner brand voice and running with what it was telling me to do.

But what was next? What was the next step towards the place and person I knew I could be?

Shifting from external approval to self-affirmation

At last, it dawned on me: external praise is fleeting. The true, enduring validation had to come from within. So, what did I do? I transformed this newfound wisdom into a fully-fledged business, holding workshops and training sessions to empower others in their brand-building, digital, and tech journeys. I took my own journey and my matured brand voice and turned it into something that could help others. I developed strategy to help the under-represented to amplify their voices and become visible through their Brand DNA and content strategies. I developed the Visibility Accelerator—a 90-day programme designed to get them visible and heard. More on that later. (Skip to part three if you want to understand the basic method to adopt to get yourself heard and visible.)

6. DIFFERENT IS YOUR SUPERPOWER

'In a world where you can be anything,
dare to be different'.

I've never settled for mediocrity. My refusal to conform became a badge of honour, a defining feature of my brand and my vision of a world that finds beauty in imperfections.

I had to go against the grain; I had to dare to be different. I started reprogramming the software running through my mind to think differently, because doing whatever everyone else was doing was not working for me. I threw out the rule book and started applying 'dare to be different' as a brand strategy to my career and life. It started back in the 2000s; slowly but surely, that's when I started seeing a shift in my own success. The key was to maintain this as my own truth, but I struggled because I was going against the norm. As I said before, post-university, I struggled to find a job. Daring to be different helped me to succeed in my career.

This pivotal career move added more weight to my overarching vision: a world where, as I've mentioned before, 'being enough' is the standard, not the exception; a world where everyone, irrespective of their backgrounds, has a fighting chance of success. At first, I tried fitting in, but of course it just didn't cut it. I was going nowhere. Instead, I was stuck in the here and now.

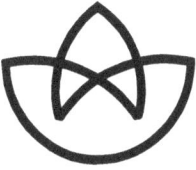

In a world where you can be anything, dare to be different.

——
VARSHA AMIN

I started to apply the 'Dare to be Different' brand strategy mantra that I lived by every day, which later turned into a movement, of sorts. This took a lot of mental strength and bravery. You know the saying, 'Nobody likes the new kid on the block'? At first, I was riddled with the fear of irrelevance, with imposter syndrome, and a lack of confidence and self-belief. What made it harder was the fact that nobody really understood me or my message. I was a nobody.

However, things really changed for me when I started experimenting with my creative mind. Then this shifted towards truly becoming limitless in what I could achieve for myself. When I stepped into me and started vocalising my own truth and being my true self, my life started changing. I got better opportunities for work; I was heard in places where I'd ordinarily been invisible; my creative talent was noticed (not by the many, but by the important few). I could now earn a living on my own terms and not be governed by the familiar past. I was designing my future world.

Rather than focusing on others and falling into a comparison trap, I want you to do the same for yourself, positioning yourself as 'different'. Because the truth is, you are unique.

Creating a difference is key to standing out, and here are five reasons why it's good to be different:

1. **Memorability:** standing out makes you unforgettable;

2. **Authenticity:** being true to yourself builds deep connections;

3. **Innovation and creativity:** thinking differently sparks innovation and creativity;

4. **Market differentiation:** carve out a unique space in your field;

5. **Adaptability and resilience:** this helps you embrace change and thrive.

You might not realise it, but everything in your life has been leading you to this moment. Your journey has shaped who you are and set the stage for a future that you can't yet imagine. Surviving life is brave, but true bravery is looking within to discover who you really are and who you can become. Let's explore this manifesto: a tailored action plan to ignite that inner flame you've been cautiously nurturing. There's a higher purpose here, a reason to help others, to pay it forward. It's time to step out of your comfort zone and arm yourself with the tools of impact.

So, how do you become a person of impact? The best way to learn is by doing. And I've been doing this for a long time, so let me guide you on your journey.

The power within

The capacity for change is already within you, so why wait for someone else to take the lead? Acknowledge your dormant potential and take control of your destiny. I'm not here to lead; I'm here to encourage you to step up and become who you're meant to be and, more importantly, who you know you're meant to be.

You are you, and that's your power'.

Your personal brand isn't crafted; it's discovered, nurtured, and unleashed. It's your innermost authenticity manifested. Authenticity can't be faked, and that's why you must be yourself. Because it's the only thing nobody else can be.

More than just a LinkedIn headline or X bio, your personal brand is your life's philosophy encapsulated. It's the story you tell the world and, more importantly, yourself. That voice that encourages you during moments of doubt? That's your authentic brand voice speaking. Aligned with your Brand DNA—your core beliefs and traits—it becomes the driving force for all you wish to achieve. Think of it as your soul's imprint on the world, your personal North Star guiding you towards a future of purpose and possibility.

Why is this important?

Because it's the bridge between your latent potential and your fulfilled self. Your personal brand empowers you

You are you, and that's your power.

VARSHA AMIN

to turn the tables, to not just lead but to inspire, innovate, and ignite change. My personal brand drives me to write these words.

I want you to hear my voice, my conviction, my truth—and spark the fire inside you. This work reflects my life's story and aims to inspire reflection on your own journey, nudging you to wield your distinctiveness as the superpower it truly is.

A kind and inclusive world for humankind

I'm building a world aligned with my core beliefs: kindness and inclusivity. Could this vision become a shared reality? I have navigated life's challenges by constantly pushing boundaries. Don't underestimate your capacity to instigate a domino effect of goodness which can uplift us all.

My vision for the future

Here's my brand vision for the future, but of course I want you to listen to the voice within and create your own vision. You're welcome to use mine as a guide or a template for your own.

I want to live in a world where:

Kindness prevails, always.

Mothers don't have to take a back seat; they always have a choice.

Leaders put their people first.

Disabilities and difficulties are not disregarded.

You're not judged if you don't excel academically.

Respect is a global currency, regardless of gender, sexuality, class, race or religion.

Algorithms bow to human intuition.

'Being enough' is a universal sentiment.

There's perfection in imperfection.

There is love and space for every living thing.

If you come from nothing, you're respected, not disrespected.

Technology is powered by humanity, allowing us to be different, uniting us all, where happiness is true wealth.

Reaching you is part of the change

Whether you're an emerging talent, a seasoned professional, or a misfit yearning for change, this book is your ally, mentor, and loudest cheerleader. You have the potential to be part of the positive change, and I want to help you achieve both your personal goals and to be instrumental in building a better world for you and humanity itself.

So, let's find out why is this so important right now. We all know the truth. It's just a case of spotlighting it.

PART TWO

WHY THE WORLD NEEDS IT

PART TWO: WHY THE WORLD NEEDS IT

To ensure a 'real world' perspective, I interviewed 12 under-represented professionals in the tech sector from across the globe, working for big tech giants through to smaller scale-ups, to gather in-depth insights, experiences and thoughts on the issues raised in my book. To ensure representation, participants ranged from the following backgrounds and ethnicities: Black African, British Indian, American Indian, White British, Afro-Caribbean, Mixed Race, Moroccan, South Indian, South Asian Canadian, Russian and Scottish. These interviews, I found, provided deep insights that validated the core messages of **Different,** particularly in relation to the key themes that I wanted to explore: personal branding, AI, challenges faced by under-represented groups, and the need for systemic change.

Let's explore the insights gained theme by theme.

1. WORKING PARENTS, PARENTHOOD AND PARENTAL LOAD

The importance of flexible work policies, especially for working parents, was a key issue raised by several participants. This supports my critique of the tech industry's lack of accommodation for working mothers, who often face the 'motherhood penalty'.

The in-depth discussion pointed out the following:

Sonal pointed out that family leave should not encroach on vacation time, and she proposed default caregiver days to help working parents avoid burnout. Of those interviewed, most of the parents said they had to take annual leave to care for a sick child—and the mothers interviewed took on the majority of the load. This often led to feelings of burnout and not having time to actually take a real break, which is cause for concern.

Reena, a mother herself, discussed how critical flexible working hours and support systems are for retaining women in the industry, particularly after they take time off for maternity leave.

Brittany reflected on how remote work during the pandemic had opened new possibilities for inclusion but also highlighted the challenges of maintaining work-life balance, particularly for working mothers.

Faith further emphasised the need for workplace policies to accommodate the realities of working mothers to prevent burnout and attrition.

Working fathers have also reported similar concerns with regards to supporting parents in the workplace. While Anthon's situation was aided by strong family support, he recognised lack of flexibility as a potential barrier. In his opinion, results-based work, not rigid hours, could mobilise more talented individuals.

Sayed acknowledged the challenges of balancing work and parenting were made more difficult without support and flexibility. Organisations should foster open discussions to better understand transitional needs, provide resources, and normalise discussions of challenges like mental health impacts and confidence issues.

Vijay's employer accommodated family responsibilities without penalty, as work-life balance and serving humanity over profits become increasingly important in a hybrid-digital future demanding re-evaluation. I believe this is the mindset and practice that every company should adopt.

2. ETHNIC MINORITIES

The systemic challenges faced by people from ethnic minorities, perhaps unsurprisingly, also emerged strongly from the interviews. These challenges back up my book's critique of the tech industry which, despite its progressive image, remains unfortunately draped in a traditional 'boys' club' mentality that marginalises people who do not fit the typical corporate mould—be that external appearance, cultural background, or perceived position in society.

The in-depth discussion pointed out the following:

Faith described her experience when working for a large oil company, where she was the only Black woman in a male-dominated tech team. She encountered pay inequality and a lack of recognition.

Suki made several points about frequently being the only brown person in the world of marketing, specifically in brand teams, working for the major UK telecoms and retail providers across circa 20 years, quoting specifically:

> *'Regarding ethnicity, the people working in Brand and Marketing didn't look like me.'*

Suki didn't face any direct discrimination or racism in the main, but she pointed out that there was one telecommunications retailer, where the head of marketing was blatantly racist towards her, and her white colleagues were treated very differently. This stood out because she'd never experienced this type of behaviour before. There had been ignorance, but she knew that her work was highly credible and she was successful, so this was cause for personal concern.

> *'And then I've worked for brands where it's either let's drop in ethnic minority or women as token representation—that's their sentiment—or let's not have them in there because it's not a reflection on our brand or the target audience, but essentially a reflection of the person in powers' personal views on what English society should look like.'*

She went on to say:

> *'I saw my other colleagues progress to senior positions in their early 30s; whether it was a man over me, or whether it was someone who was not brown or black, I've seen their career path rewarded. Through sheer grit and determination, I eventually became a marketing director in my late 40s'. It should have happened earlier, but I didn't consistently have fair line managers who, sadly for myself, knew what not doing the right thing looked like and were OK with using me, but not promoting my highly commendable work ethics, people management and significant contribution towards company profits and positive reputation with industry leads.'*

Suki also pointed out that companies don't need to be 'woke' and jumping on the diversity bandwagon as such, as often it's not genuine. It is better to focus on recruiting the best person for the job and promoting those whom you don't want to lose, as they add so much value. So, getting quotas up for diversity's sake is the wrong thing to do.

When asked, Is the tech industry a white boys' club? Suki explained:

> 'Yes, I completely agree with that statement. I have mainly had male bosses above me and 70% have been brilliant line managers. I've seen them progress me, support me, but then I've seen the other side—and still pretty recently—where I was not being promoted, and it was clearly visible by my colleagues. And people who were 15 years younger than me— something like that—starting off in their careers, were given higher job titles than me.
>
> There is clearly a mentality of use and not promote, if your face doesn't 'fit' or you are indirectly causing jealousy or seen as a threat to insecure others. I have always felt my ethnicity and upbringing has instilled an extremely hard-working mentality and I wouldn't change it for the world, but it needs recognition and appreciation. I have again recently been told I could have been promoted but, reading between the lines, the reason was again the glass ceiling—there is a white male member of the team who is four years older than me so 'it wouldn't look right to him'. I am flabbergasted... My CEO is a white male and I am three years older than him so, that's deemed as OK, clearly.'

Reflecting the experience described above, Sonal shared her early career experience as an ethnic minority person in tech, where she often felt it was hard to stand out, particularly as a remote worker.

Soukayna, too, reflected on the discrimination she faced, particularly from a past manager, where she felt undervalued because of her background. She also pointed to persistent issues like gender pay gaps and the lack of women in leadership roles as clear indicators of the systemic barriers still in place.

Reena, who has long worked in the tech industry, shared her frustration at being consistently sidelined for promotions despite her qualifications—a story that echoes my discussion about how systemic biases prevent many women of colour from advancing in their careers.

Francis, who is Scottish, described instances of hatred based on his background when south of the border, and though never having been discriminated against or treated badly professionally, he did feel that white minorities in Britain are intrinsically perceived as different to the 'Anglo Saxon' majority population in England. As such, he felt that people from white minority backgrounds could stand as empathetic allies to those of more externally obvious marginalised groups. He pointed out that the lack of riots in Scotland (referring to the racially motivated incidents in England, August 2024) were another indicator of the fact that Scottish people, on the whole, not only have a distaste for racism, but themselves may feel a connection with under-represented groups.

Anthon shared experiences of feeling overlooked and undervalued in previous corporate roles, which he partly attributed to unconscious bias. Though now more confident in his abilities, he still sometimes feels isolated as the only person from his background within teams.

Sayed shared his experience of facing unconscious bias and feeling undervalued early in his career due to his ethnic background. He felt pressure to constantly prove himself and work harder than peers to succeed. While progress has been made, he believes more can be done to advance representation and reduce gender pay gaps, particular for ethnic minority workers.

Vijay mentioned that while representation inspires, forced inclusion damages authentic storytelling. Under-represented communities deserve opportunities naturally fitting their histories. Meaningfully, Vijay stated:

> *'New voices emerge through accessible information, not tokenism.'*

3. NEURODIVERSITY

Unsurprisingly, the systemic challenges faced by neurodiverse individuals also emerged strongly from the interviews, but not by those who were necessarily neurodiverse themselves. In all honesty, I struggled with people not wanting to come forward to talk openly about their neurodiversity. I fear that this is still a subject that people are uncomfortable talking about openly, and regrettably it's why there is still low awareness in companies. But the fact that people don't feel a sense of belonging and want to hide their neurodiversity in the workplace is because they don't feel safe raising it, believing they are going to be perceived in a certain way by the world. This thinking needs to change, and as a community we must think of neurodiversity positively, because I think that the positives outweigh the perceived negatives.

A new report has claimed that neurodivergence is massively underestimated in the technology industry. A report by Diversity in Tech[8], published in 2024 by the non-profit organisation Tech Talent Charter (TTC), revealed shockingly low reported levels of neurodivergent people working in tech. According to the report, 53% of employees identify as neurodiverse, but employers believe the proportion is only 3%. This disconnect reveals a deeper problem: the industry's

---

[8]   Diversity In Tech. Accessed January 2025: https://www.techtalentcharter.co.uk/reports/diversity-in-tech-report-2024/

failure to fully acknowledge and embrace diverse talents and perspectives. This is not OK.

As I reflect on this, it's clear that simply waiting for change isn't enough. Our personal brands can be the catalyst for driving this much-needed shift. When we embrace and amplify our unique identities, we create space for conversations that challenge the status quo. Your personal brand is a powerful tool—it's your voice, your story, and your platform for advocating change. By speaking up about your own experiences, sharing insights, and championing the value of diversity, you influence the narrative and make others see the importance of inclusion.

4. LGBTQ+

Representing all voices was no doubt going to be a challenge throughout this book, but I will speak from the perspectives of those individuals within the LGBTQ+ communities that I interviewed and how they have been treated in the workplace. While the world isn't comfortable about talking about these truths even in 2025, many people are realising the power of true inclusivity. There is still so much that needs to change if we're to build a kinder and more inclusive world.

The in-depth discussion highlighted the following:

Jonny pointed out that he has become more comfortable being his authentic self at work over time, though he is selective about when and with whom he discloses his sexual orientation. He has experienced some challenges in the past where he felt that he needed to conform to stereotypes, but he has worked towards being his true self.

Jonny has felt the challenges of being an under-represented minority in tech. At times he has felt that he is not taken as seriously as others, though he is unsure if this is directly tied to his sexual orientation or other factors. He notes that the tech industry can be competitive and aggressive, and that he has sometimes felt the need to 'bark louder' to have his voice heard, which he acknowledges is not an ideal approach.

In a world increasingly shaped by GenAI, it's crucial that tech companies authentically represent the LGBTQ+ community to ensure inclusivity in the products and systems they create. AI systems learn from the data they are fed, and if that data lacks diversity, it will perpetuate existing biases. By embracing the LGBTQ+ community and reflecting their voices and experiences, tech companies can create more equitable and representative solutions.

Your personal brand, when built with authenticity and purpose, can be a powerful force in shaping the future of the tech industry. By standing for inclusivity, advocating for under-represented groups, and leading by example, you help to push the industry towards a future where technology serves everyone, not just a select few.

5. LEADERSHIP, MENTORSHIP AND ALLYSHIP

Mentorship and allyship were also strong themes in the interviews, with many participants attributing their career progression to the support of mentors and allies who helped them along the way.

The in-depth discussion pointed out the following:

Sonal credited the 'I Am Remarkable' programme with empowering her to advocate for her strengths and noted that mentorship played an essential role in her personal growth. She stressed that having mentors who were invested in her success was the key to improved future opportunities.

Soukayna, who benefitted from having supportive managers at Google, highlighted how diverse leadership and allyship foster a culture of representation and retention.

Francis also discussed how the mentorship he received early in his career helped him understand the importance of visibility and self-promotion.

Reena echoed these sentiments, noting that without her mentors, navigating the biases of the tech industry as a woman of colour would have been far more difficult.

Suki pointed out that allyship at the leadership level is essential, stating that leaders could actively sponsor and advocate for those who are under-represented to drive meaningful change, but only if they believe in the purpose themselves. It has to be real and from within. A great example of this is a female white woman, who has lived and breathed allyship in Suki's career as her line manager in three roles to date over a nearly 30-year career. This woman has built diverse teams in such a natural way and doesn't see colour, age or gender. Furthermore, she has been an inspirational role model to Suki, and reminded her that she is indeed British born, proudly English and isn't different but unique, bringing culture and diversity; that home isn't assumed as India, it's London, UK. She added:

> *'Being Indian makes me different, but allyship makes it a special part of you, not a barrier to progression.'*

Brittany shared how her mentor helped her to build the confidence and network that she needed to advance to leadership roles, while Faith reflected on how a mentoring circle had taught her the importance of visibility and advocacy, particularly as a woman in tech.

Victoria reflected on the valuable mentorship she received early in her career that helped her to navigate cultural differences and gain confidence. She also highlighted the importance of mental health support in the workplace, noting the differences in awareness and resources between Russia and the UK, and the benefits of having a supportive community.

From a leadership perspective, Victoria noted her experience of nepotism pointing out the following:

> *'It's a scenario I see time and time again, unfortunately. When a company grows rapidly and transitions into a larger corporation, senior leadership often start hiring their friends. Now, I'm not against bringing someone on board if you've had a positive working experience with them in the past—that can be a smart move. However, I strongly disagree with prioritising personal relationships over expertise. Opportunities should be open to everyone and filled by the person best suited for the role, whether they're your mate or not.'*

While allyship and leadership are important, I have also seen the other side of this, when a CEO said to me, *'You're too expensive for the role.'* And this was despite hiring me at my asking salary, which to be fair was much below where I should have been. I wonder if he would have said that to me if I was a white male in my 50s?

I think we all know the answer to that.

You should know your worth and go to environments where people see your worth. Shortly after that conversation, I was offered a position that was £30k a year more than what this particular CEO was offering me.

If anything, it was clear that I was being short-changed. Was it because I was a young woman of colour? Again, we all know the truth. Thankfully, my personal brand helped me to land my next lucrative opportunity, and so can yours.

Clearly there's so much work that needs to be done here as this is not OK.

6. PERSONAL BRANDING

Nearly every participant acknowledged the power of personal branding as a tool for empowerment and success— with varying flavours and approaches.

The in-depth discussion pointed out the following:

Sonal, reflecting on her career, discussed how essential it was to build networks, do your job well, take constructive feedback and learn from mistakes. She pointed out that authenticity and advocating for oneself were integral to personal branding and career progression, aligning closely with my opinion that personal branding is so much more than self-promotion. In fact, showcasing your authentic identity can help you stand out.

Victoria discussed how developing her personal brand had helped elevate her voice and expertise, allowing her to share her knowledge and connect with others in her field. She emphasised the importance of personal branding, especially for under-represented groups, as a way to take control of one's narrative and showcase your unique value.

Soukayna also illustrated this point, sharing how her decision to start wearing a hijab at Google became part of her personal branding journey. Her identity and the authenticity she brought to the workplace allowed her to advocate for under-represented groups lacking role models, which was a huge part of her career development (with the bonus of having a positive social effect). She recently also pointed out in her own LinkedIn post:

> *'As a Muslim woman, once you take the decision to start covering your hair, you'll be perceived differently. It's up to you to use that as a strength or insecurity. The truth is, people will be their nicest to you when you fit a common definition or stereotype. Once you step back from that definition, be ready to be perceived differently.'*

Similarly, Francis explained how he built his brand around his technical skills and work ethic, positioning himself as a reliable and skilled professional.

Reena used her brand to highlight her unique strengths as a woman of colour in tech, helping her to stand out despite systemic barriers.

Suki pointed out that her brand evolved around resilience and adaptability, and for personal branding, which meant using her story to connect with others and unlock new opportunities. She has also managed circa 40 individuals as her direct reports, including graduates and apprentices. She prides herself that best practices have been used, and succession planning is imperative to empower, recognise and reward hard-working employees. Everything missing from her own path is undertaken and the positives are also used for the benefit of others. This has resulted in teams that highly respect Suki and do her proud in every role (Suki gets the reward), but it has always reminded her of the 30% of line managers who have let her and their company down on the implementation of diversity, equity and inclusion (DEI) practices.

Anthon believed that personal branding was vital for entrepreneurs to showcase their expertise and build trust.

Faith spoke at length about how defining her brand around empowering women in tech advocacy opened opportunities, such as her representation at the United Nations (UN).

Sayed emphasised building an authentic personal brand true to oneself, rather than becoming something not genuine to fit in. While uncomfortable promoting himself, he understood the importance of using his platform to help others.

But from those who understand the value of brand, very few understand how they can embrace the power that GenAI has, to power their voice. GenAI can turn your voice into content creation, which allows you to distribute your branded content to your audience with precision.

7. GENERATIVE AI, AUTOMATION AND AUGMENTATION

Last, but not least, the role of technology as both a tool for progress and a potential source of inequity, was a recurring theme in the interviews.

The in-depth discussion pointed out the following:

Soukayna expressed optimism about how technology, particularly platforms like LinkedIn, could level opportunities for under-represented groups. She encouraged individuals to focus on developing skills that complement technological advancements to stay competitive.

Sonal noted that technology could scale one's message and productivity exponentially if used thoughtfully, but she cautioned that it should always be coupled with authenticity.

Brittany pointed out how technology can amplify personal brands and open up new opportunities, particularly for those who are otherwise marginalised.

Francis acknowledged the risks posed by AI and automation, particularly the displacement of jobs held by women, but he also highlighted the potential for new opportunities if proper skills training is provided.

Reena raised concerns about the digital divide, noting that while technology has made remote work more accessible, it has also highlighted the disparities in access to necessary tools and resources for certain under-represented groups.

Suki relayed that AI and automation could either open doors or close them, depending on whether individuals receive the right training and support. AI apps like ChatGPT should not replace ideas and execution that we enjoy from real people and their personalities, which utilise their education, experience and intelligence.

Faith added that while AI can aid content creation, it cannot replace the human qualities of storytelling and lived experience, which remain vital in roles like coaching.

Vijay also added that AI augments, but humans understand context and build relationships. Jobs will change, not disappear, yet universal basic income may become necessary if worklessness spreads. Progress demands considering all.

Anthon viewed AI as augmenting but not replacing his data analysis and consulting work, requiring human guidance and relationships. He was not threatened by AI due to the enduring need for strategic and emotional skills.

Sayed believed that AI should be embraced to enhance rather than replace human roles. With curiosity and understanding, AI can streamline learning and help refine ideas. As technology evolves, the focus should remain on serving human needs and exploring what it means to be human.

Jonny referenced using AI tools all the time to help with his personal life, and AI image generating to help him with work and personal life. He quotes that he uses ChatGPT on his mobile to help him flesh out ideas for his recipe reels on Instagram. Jonny shared examples of how he has used AI tools like image generation and text summarisation to assist with his work, although he had some concerns about the potential long-term impact of AI on creative roles. He sees AI as a useful tool in the short-term but is wary of over-reliance on it.

In contrast, Victoria expressed a positive outlook on the impact of GenAI, seeing it as a tool to enhance her work rather than replace her.

All participants acknowledged that AI could augment their work, for example by helping them to better draft emails at work or to summarise lengthy documents.

These diverse voices provide further validation for the key themes explored in my book. Personal branding, parental load, systemic barriers, mentorship, allyship, the impact AI can have, and the need for collective action, remain at the very core of driving the changes necessary to create a more inclusive and equitable tech industry and, ultimately, world.

8. WHAT CAN BE DONE TO REVERSE UNDER-REPRESENTATION?

Well, amplifying diverse voices is an essential step. This involves creating platforms and opportunities for under-represented groups to share their ideas, insights, and experiences—like this book.

In the tech industry, this means offering up more speaking opportunities at conferences to personal brands that are under-represented, leadership roles in key projects, or representation in decision-making bodies. Amplifying diverse voices not only enriches the conversation but also helps to break down stereotypes and foster a culture of inclusion.

Beyond these steps, there are several other ways to promote equity, inclusion and diversity in the workplace:

1. **Education and awareness:** Continuous education and awareness-raising about the benefits of diversity and the challenges faced by under-represented groups are essential. This can involve training sessions, workshops, and discussions that foster a deeper understanding of diversity and inclusion issues.

2. **Mentorship and sponsorship programmes:** These programmes can provide invaluable support to minority employees. Mentors and sponsors can offer guidance, share their experiences, and help open doors to new opportunities.

3. **Diverse hiring practices:** Companies need to ensure that their hiring practices are fair and inclusive. This can involve using diverse hiring panels, removing bias from job descriptions, and actively seeking candidates from a range of backgrounds.

4. **Supportive policies and practices:** Developing policies and practices that support a diverse workforce is crucial. This can include flexible working arrangements, generous parental leave policies, and robust support for mental health and wellbeing.

5. **Inclusive leadership:** Leaders play a critical role in fostering an inclusive culture. This involves leading by example, being open to feedback, and being willing to make changes to support diversity and inclusion.

6. **Community engagement:** Engaging with the broader community can help companies understand the needs and perspectives of different groups. This can involve partnerships with community organisations, participation in community events, or support for community initiatives.

It goes without saying, however, that achieving true diversity and inclusion in the workplace requires a sustained and concerted effort—not just paying lip service. It's not just about implementing a few policies or initiatives; it's about creating a culture where diversity and inclusion and a sense of belonging are valued and embedded in every aspect of the organisation, and culture at large. It involves everyone.

So, while progress has been made, there is still a lot of work to be done to achieve equity, inclusion and true diversity in the workplace, particularly in the tech sector.

So where do we fit into this puzzle?

How does my personal brand (and yours) have the potential to help others?

You and I, as our authentic selves—how do we make our voices heard?

Let's find out.

PART THREE

HOW YOU CAN DO IT

PART THREE: HOW YOU CAN DO IT

To get to the point where you are comfortable sharing your story, your message, and are then being listened to, requires some thought and strategy. For those people who think that brand strategy isn't essential, let me tell you this: without your brand strategy, your brand will not command the attention or premium that it deserves. So, let's start with your Brand DNA, a framework that is easy to apply and will become your blueprint.

1. YOUR BRAND STRATEGY — BRAND DNA

Who are you, and why do you exist beyond your titles and making money?

If you don't know yet, start with your story, as I started with mine. Your highs and lows up until this point will reveal this to you. I define this as your Brand DNA; it's the connection you have with your higher-self, your story, and the significance it holds for others. If you truly want change, this is what it will look like.

Be brave enough to listen to your own voice. If you still need an external force by your side, remember I'm unequivocally by your side.

Start with your story, as it forms the basis of your brand narrative. Your why is embedded here, you just need to tease this out—sometimes with help or with time. That bolt of clarity will descend precisely when you're ready for it. Trust the process and the timing.

So, what are the key components for building a strong personal brand? It all starts with your purpose.

Why do you exist?

Beyond financial gain, my personal mantra is:

> *'I rise to lift others.'*

This is what gets me out of bed every day—to serve others. I do this with kindness in mind; to make the world a kinder place. That's my vision. I do it by serving those that I can with the limited time that I have, being a mother of two young children, a wife, a sister, a daughter, and a freelance founder, having had exceptional corporate career success, too.

More importantly, at the core of my being is 'seva' (which means to serve in Gujarati) those people who feel marginalised; those who are currently under-represented in technology; those who need to be heard, and for the personal brands that need amplification, now that brand amplification can be powered by AI.

My problem is that I have lots of competing responsibilities. I want to do more great things, but I've come to realise that you can't burden yourself with everything all at once. There's a time and place for everything. You have to trust the process and yourself—even when everyone else is telling you otherwise.

Don't listen to the gurus who say that you have to post content seven days a week, and develop reels and videos continuously, and be brilliant at everything else. The truth is, that is not sustainable. It will only lead to digital and mental burnout.

Instead, you have to get smart about the things that matter the most. This is about protecting your mental health. You have to set boundaries, and say no even when it's a difficult or unpopular choice. Trust your intuition, too—it really doesn't lie—and don't get distracted.

You don't have to grind; you just have to be laser-focussed in your brand-building efforts. There is no point speaking to an audience that doesn't speak your language. They won't turn up, and they won't be engaged. So, the key is to go where you're relevant.

But to be relevant you need to firstly understand:

- Why you exist as a personal brand beyond making money (your current state);

- What you do (your expertise + authority);

- How you do it (your skills, services and product ecosystem),

- Where you're heading (your future state).

I couldn't find a visual that demonstrated my words, so I created my own version of the truth. If this helps you, please use it to first define who you really are and what you stand for, ahead of sharing your message with the world.

You'll thank yourself later.

Brand DNA Blueprint

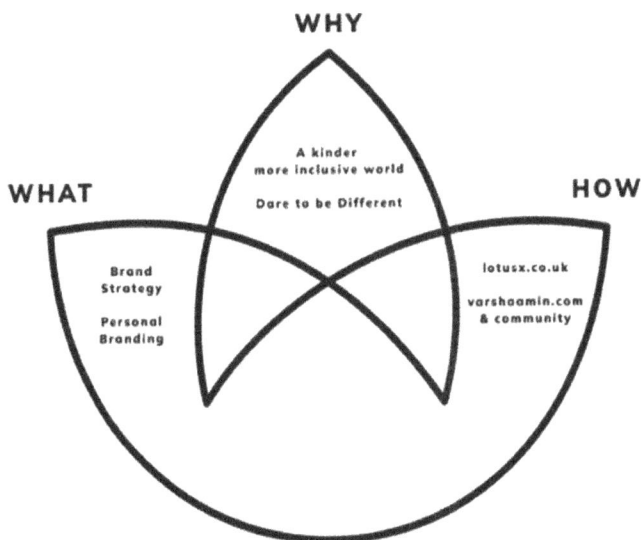

WHY

WHAT

HOW

A kinder
more inclusive world

Dare to be Different

Brand
Strategy

Personal
Branding

lotusx.co.uk

varshaamin.com
& community

WHY I DO WHAT I DO:

- I exist to build a kinder and inclusive world

- Everyone should be seen and heard

- Our differences should be celebrated—so, **Dare to be Different**

WHAT I DO:

- Brand strategy and brand marketing for corporates in tech, innovation, and AI

- Personal branding: I brand and represent the under-represented in tech, innovation, and AI

- Tech, digital and personal branding skills training for working parents, entrepreneurs, coaches and corporates

HOW I SERVE:

- varshaamin.com (Personal Brand Strategist)

- Lotusx.co.uk (training + coaching)

- Different Community (see below)

MY FUTURE STATE

The Different Community is more than a pillar of my brand—it's the heartbeat of everything I stand for. This space is designed to elevate under-represented voices in tech, empowering individuals to own their uniqueness and use it as a superpower. Together, we'll dismantle barriers, rewrite the narrative, and amplify the potential of those who have been overlooked for far too long.

Through connection and collaboration, the Different Community becomes a platform where we share strategies, insights, and stories, building a network that fosters growth and resilience.

For under-represented individuals, this community offers visibility, validation, and a chance to amplify their voice in a crowded space. We'll harness the power of personal branding to not just level the playing field but to redefine it. By sharing our journeys, we'll create ripple effects that inspire others to do the same.

As the community grows, so does its power to amplify brands—individually and collectively. Whether through mentoring, collaborations or leveraging AI to tell our stories, the Different Community is where authenticity meets impact, reshaping tech and paving the way for a fairer, brighter and more inclusive future.

My message and brand strategy: Dare to be Different

This is a philosophy, mantra, and movement but more importantly, a cultural element to how I live my life. It is interlinked with everything I do and say, the actions I take, and how I make others feel, the products I launch, and the brands that I decide to work with. It helps me to exclude everything that does not serve me.

In everything that I do, I question originality, because otherwise I'm not doing justice to myself. It's about being brave and bold, doing what nobody has done before. There's no fun in copying anyone. You are uniquely different; your

DNA sets you apart, as does everything else about you. So why are we so busy trying to be like everyone else? It's because we care so much about what everyone else thinks of us.

It's time to remove those fears and take a plunge into the unknown, to navigate those dark and murky waters. Just know that you will come out the other end, conquering your own inner universe and most likely the external world, too. They'll see you then, if they haven't seen you yet.

But before they see you, you have to be clear on your audience.

Who are you serving and what is the significance of this?

Start with picking one key audience, as the beauty of this is that you'll stay really focussed. My audience is basically people like me—extremely driven, change-makers, talented in their profession, but who really don't get the limelight that they truly deserve. Let me explain what this looks like.

My audience:

- Under-represented and diverse voices that don't get heard and don't get the visibility they deserve.

- Working parents, entrepreneurs, CEOs, CMOs, coaches and consultants from under-represented groups, the neurodiverse in tech.

- They are time poor but cash rich; they need nurturing.

- Location: global.

- Their primary brand archetype is 'the creator'. Typical corporate organisations that fall into this include Apple, Adobe, Lego, and Crayola. I will explain what this means later and in the context of personal branding.

Brand narrative

Your brand narrative is interwoven into your story: what you stand for, and what you're trying to change in the world. My narrative talks to all the people out there who are aspiring to be pioneers and trailblazers. Those people who do not conform, to those who believe in originality; more importantly, they are creators and innovators. They are not dinosaurs from a prehistoric era; they are forward-thinkers, progressive, and purpose-led individuals. They are exceptionally creative and bright—not textbook types. They tend to rewrite the rules to improve things; they can see the white spaces and the gaps, even when they aren't obvious to others. In other words, they are mostly guided by their intuition.

This is where knowing your primary brand archetype is so important as a personal brand. The type that you are, will help you to speak in a universal language that attracts the right type of people to your brand—those who believe in what you believe in.

Brand archetypes

Carl Jung, a Swiss psychiatrist, developed a set of 12 archetypes, referring to patterns of thought present in all humans. The archetypes offer a way to position your personal brand and business brand with purpose, aligning your message to resonate more deeply with your audience. By identifying the right archetype, you can harness the power of branding to amplify its impact.

These are summarised below:

1. **The Innocent.** Optimistic and pure, this archetype values simplicity, goodness, and happiness. Brands like this are often seen as honest and wholesome, promoting a message of positivity and trust.

2. **The Explorer.** Driven by a desire for adventure and freedom, the Explorer seeks discovery and new experiences. These brands encourage breaking boundaries and embracing the unknown.

3. **The Sage.** Focused on knowledge and wisdom, the Sage archetype strives to share insight and uncover the truth. Brands aligned with the Sage are seen as trustworthy sources of information and guidance.

4. **The Hero.** The Hero archetype is all about courage, strength and determination. These brands inspire people to overcome challenges and achieve greatness, often embodying boldness and action.

5. **The Outlaw.** Rebellious and disruptive, the Outlaw seeks to break the rules and challenge the status quo. Brands under this archetype embrace change and inspire a sense of revolution and freedom.

6. **The Magician.** Transformational and visionary, the Magician archetype focuses on making dreams come true and creating change. These brands often appear innovative and focus on creating extraordinary results.

7. **The Lover.** All about connection and passion, the Lover archetype seeks to create intimate relationships and emotional connections. Brands that fall under this category evoke desire, beauty and pleasure.

8. **The Jester.** Fun-loving and spontaneous, the Jester archetype lives to entertain and bring joy. Brands like this are playful, light-hearted, and focus on making people smile.

9. **The Caregiver.** Empathetic and nurturing, the Caregiver archetype is driven by the desire to protect and care for others. These brands are compassionate, offering support, care and reassurance.

10. **The Ruler.** Powerful and authoritative, the Ruler archetype craves control and stability. Brands in this category are seen as leaders, striving for order and excellence.

11. **The Creator.** The Creator values imagination, innovation, and self-expression. These brands are often visionary, encouraging creativity and bringing new ideas to life.

12. **The Everyman.** Relatable and grounded, the Everyman archetype is all about belonging and community. These brands are approachable, genuine, and strive to connect with everyone on a human level.

You've probably guessed by now which type I fall into. Although I have elements of several types (as many brands do), my primary archetype is the Creator.

Take a look and decide which one your brand is most like. If you're struggling, feel free to reach out to me, as I'd be happy to help. But be prepared, because it is a process where I go into detail about your past, I move you into the present moment and then help you to define what your future brand looks like. It's a co-produced plan to get you seen, heard and visible to the relevant brands and even to corporate identities.

This process will help you to attract the right employers and the right prospective customers. But more importantly, it's a retention strategy too. If you get this right, even when things don't go to plan, the roots and foundations of your inner lotus will be so robust that nothing will bring you down.

The Lotus, as in you, will continue to bloom.

Here are some diverse personalities who, like me, align with the Creator archetype, and each one is known for breaking barriers and driving innovation:

1. **Timnit Gebru** – a pioneering AI researcher and advocate for ethical AI, particularly in highlighting the biases in AI systems. She is a strong voice for diversity and accountability in the tech industry.

2. **Reshma Saujani** – the founder of Girls Who Code, Reshma is an innovator focused on closing the gender gap in technology by empowering young women to pursue careers in coding and tech.

3. **Victor Tsaran** – an accessibility engineer and advocate for people with disabilities in the tech space. Victor has worked on improving digital accessibility at companies like Google and PayPal, helping to shape more inclusive technology.

4. **Anne-Marie Imafidon** – as the founder of Stemettes, she's been a trailblazer in promoting women and under-represented groups in STEM fields.

5. **Bozoma Saint John** – a dynamic marketing leader who has worked for companies like Uber, Apple and Netflix. She is known for her creative strategies and advocacy for diversity in tech and marketing.

6. **Nishma Patel Robb** – a seasoned marketing leader in the tech industry, she has held roles such as Director of Brand and Reputation Marketing at Google. Nishma is known for her innovative approaches to marketing strategy and her dedication to diversity, inclusion, and the empowerment of under-represented communities in tech.

These personalities have made significant impacts in both tech and creative spheres, often through innovative approaches to marketing and branding while championing diversity and inclusivity.

So, let's get to the point. By using my Brand DNA blueprint as a guide, you should be able to identify your brand archetype; have clarity on the theme that runs through your story to turn it into a message. What next?

You need a method, a framework, to get you there.

2. THE 3-STEP VISIBILITY METHOD

As you will have been able to see from my story, life has been a tireless tutor for me, a blend of highs, lows and the grit in between. How could I take these rich lessons and make them actionable for others? Enter the Visibility Accelerator—a distillation of my life's wisdom, designed to guide you through the maze of personal branding in this AI era. Because that's what this is all about, taking who I've become and passing it on to you; the next step in creating a better version of you and giving you the skillset and mindset to take that further into the world.

The Visibility Accelerator pivots around three fundamental elements, each crucial for amplifying your personal brand:

Brand Triangle

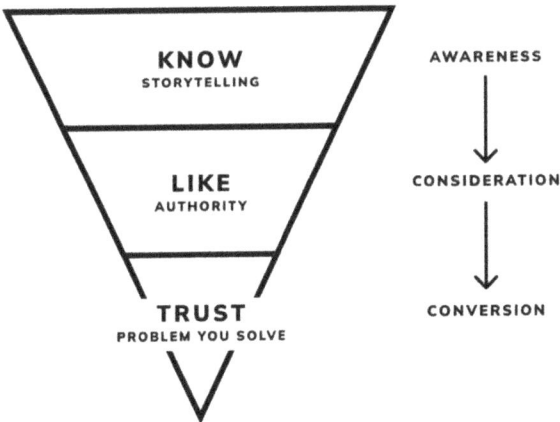

1. **KNOW:** This where your narrative morphs into your brand's story, the product of which is your Brand DNA. Here, you'll master the art of crafting content that speaks to your audience, thus elevating your visibility. This, in the traditional sense, is brand awareness.

2. **LIKE:** This happens through your content strategy. Once your brand crystallises, what's next? Drawing in an audience. But not just any crowd—a community that resonates with your values and vision. This is where you talk about your expertise and work towards becoming an authority in your niche. Mine is brand strategy for tech and how you leverage AI to amplify your brand.

3. **TRUST:** The ultimate aim is conversion, but what does that really mean? It's about morphing your heightened visibility into tangible outcomes, be it new job prospects, client relationships, partnerships or building a community. Here the focus should be on the problems that you can solve for your prospective employers and even existing or new clients.

The soul of brand awareness: beyond metrics

When we speak of brand awareness, it's tempting to reduce it to simply numbers or social media statistics. Surely that's what business is all about. But isn't it far more? I would argue that it absolutely is. It's the heartbeat of your brand—your shared stories, values, and the emotional chords you strike with your audience. This is your stage to engage in storytelling, capturing not just eyeballs but hearts. You see, people aren't just buying into a product or a service; they're buying into you and me—our authenticity.

A journey grounded in authenticity

Let's not forget, the Visibility Accelerator is a journey. I've designed it to be this way, based on my own experiences and evolution. Each step is laced with lessons from my own life—about surmounting odds, tackling challenges and, above all, being my own catalyst for change. After all, in the quest for a stronger brand and a better world, we are our most potent ally.

This is what elevates the Visibility Accelerator from other branding services; it's the personal touch interwoven into each phase, with an element of mindset reprogramming to give you the courage to start. You're journeying with me, learning from my highs and lows, trials and triumphs. This is a tailor-made experience, imbued with wisdom and insights that I have accrued over the years.

Personal branding—summed up

Building a strong personal brand is an essential strategy for professionals and entrepreneurs seeking to establish themselves in their respective fields. A personal brand is a unique combination of skills, experiences and personality that you want the world to see in you. It's about how you present yourself to others, and how you're perceived in the marketplace. A strong personal brand can lead to many opportunities, including career advancement, industry recognition and networking possibilities.

In the tech world, opportunities are abundant, but they are not distributed equally. The landscape is such that visibility often becomes a crucial factor in determining who gets access to these opportunities. This is where personal branding comes into play, acting as a catalyst that propels individuals from the periphery to the centre stage. Personal branding is not just about self-promotion; it's a strategic approach to ensuring that your skills, experience and insights gain the recognition they deserve.

Remaining in the shadows can mean missed opportunities, but personal brand building provides the platform to showcase your expertise and thought leadership, making you a visible and influential figure in your field. More important than influence, it is the impact you can make on other's lives.

'Be brave enough to listen to your own brand voice.'

If your brand's core purpose is strong, and the foundations of your inner lotus are strong, then you're going to end up in the right direction eventually, because the only way is up, even if you don't yet have the words to make it meaningful to you or others.

'Don't overthink it, just start. Iterate, update, and evolve along the way.'

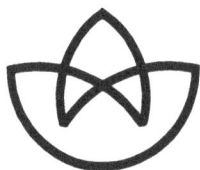

Be brave enough to listen to your own brand voice.

VARSHA AMIN

Brands evolve, as do people, so you don't have to have it all figured out now.

Other key things to consider:

Don't fake it. Authenticity is the cornerstone of a personal brand. It means being true to who you are, your values and your beliefs. Authenticity is about showing your genuine self to the world, rather than projecting an image that you think others want to see. This genuine approach builds trust and reliability in your professional or business network. I share my personal stories through LinkedIn posts, and they essentially align to my brand's DNA. I highlight all the things that are important to my brand, including kindness, inclusivity, and parenthood. I find that these posts build emotional connections with my community and in many cases go viral. Authenticity is a crucial component to getting our differences accepted and celebrated.

Consistency. Consistency in your message, and how you present yourself is crucial. This includes consistently communicating your brand across various platforms and maintaining the same tone, style and values. Consistency helps in building recognition and makes your brand more memorable. Committing to consistency can be challenging at times but remember that the more people who are exposed to your message, the faster you can build your personal brand. Given that I must divide my time between raising my family and working, I can commit to posting on LinkedIn once or twice a week.

> For example: I spend a few hours in the evenings formulating my content, and I schedule it to go out a week in advance so that I'm not panicking about being consistent. You can do the same. Even if it means you're only posting once a week or once a month, the key is to build this into a habit. Remember that it takes time and effort to build a quality brand. If you struggle to set some time aside, block out a one to two-hour slot each week. I use bullet points to put together my ideas, based on the method—story, expertise, and how to solve a problem—then I use AI to give me 10 post choices for the month ahead, based on my tone of voice and writing style. The output usually isn't that great, so it needs me to inject my own creativity. But what previously took me five hours, I can now do in one to two hours.

What makes you different? Your brand's value is what sets you apart from others. It's about understanding what unique skills, experiences or perspectives you bring to the table. This could be specialised knowledge, distinctive skills or even unique ways of solving problems. Clearly articulating your value makes you more attractive to potential employers, clients or collaborators.

> For example: This is where I tend to post about my expertise and knowledge across brand strategies, digital innovation, and technology. Whilst this type of content ranks lower in engagement compared to my storytelling posts, it helps you to emphasise credibility in your niche. This type of content tends to generate leads in the longer term. I use a blend of emotional storytelling, thought-provoking posts, and posts that are related to new technologies or strategies that help to build my brand.

Visibility. Being visible is about putting yourself out there and being seen and heard. This means actively showcasing your skills, knowledge and experiences to the world. Increased visibility raises your profile and can open up new opportunities.

> For example: Don't just take my word for it. Just by showing up continuously and writing content around my audience's needs, I was given the opportunity to be featured on BBC tech news as well as being shortlisted and invited to deliver a personal branding workshop for under-represented groups at one of the

world's biggest tech giants, Adobe, in London. Even when you're sharing your content and you get zero reactions or shares, believe it or not people are noticing, watching, and thinking about you. You have their share of mind, because you have a strong share of brand voice, just by consistently being visible. This is what I would define as an 'always-on-brand' strategy. This works for both a business brand and a personal brand.

How to brand organically

You don't need to run paid ads; you can build your brand organically—you just need to be willing to put in the work. It's a slow and steady approach and can take up to 12 months to get heard, but the benefits are worth it.

I believe that this has given me a competitive advantage when it comes to recruitment selection for those employers who don't know me yet. Your personal brand will become a vital asset in future-proofing your career, or when building your business. And if you're a Gen-Zer, you'll need this skill more than ever to land your future role at a company that matches your vision and values. If you don't have any experience, then dial up your expertise in the area where you want to be.

> For example: If you're doing a digital marketing role and want to pivot to a digital strategy role, my advice would be to start owning this space and upskilling yourself in this area, then working to demonstrate this

newfound intelligence to show your manager or prospective employer just what is possible. The same goes for if you're setting up a business. Become a master in your niche and create a strong point of difference in your offer and brand positioning.

Throughout my career my personal brand has also led to organisations wanting to write about me. For example, Gamma for International Women's Day 2022 and Simplyhealth in 2020 featured my personal brand across internal corporate comms after I was featured on BBC tech news. This instantly raised my profile. I must admit that I do struggle with self-promotion at times because I prefer to remain humble and out of the spotlight. So let others speak of your talent.

It's what others say about you when you're absent from that meeting room that matters. That's why champions and allies are so crucial in helping not only to build a strong personal brand, but they really have the ability to *amplify* your brand.

If nobody is willing to advocate for you, then your voice doesn't have the same impact. A bunch of advocates—in other words Brand Amplifiers—are humans who care. And they have great power and responsibility. This allows you to scale your visibility organically; see these connections as your way to reach more people and build your community, illustrated next.

Connected Circles

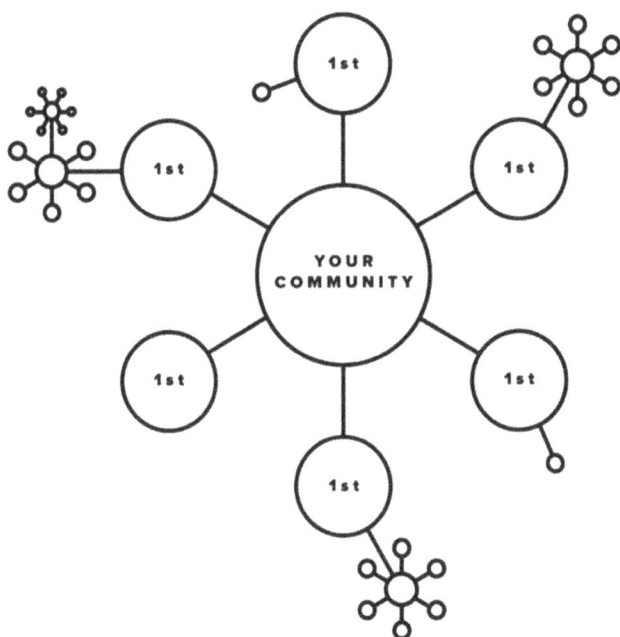

These connections are extremely valuable, each of them connects to a person who cares about what you stand for. As a result, they are likely to attach an emotional connection with you. This is when the magic happens—when they engage with you, they help you to amplify your message as they have their own micro-communities that are highly likely to resonate with your message too. This creates broader brand amplification, helping you reach more people without needing to spend money on advertising. That said, it's important to build strong relationships with these people.

Attracting true advocates

Focus on attracting fans who genuinely believe in your brand and will advocate for you. These are not just followers, but are people who will actively share your content, refer you to others, and support your brand initiatives. Engaging with your advocates and nurturing these relationships can lead to a loyal and supportive network and connections.

> For example: I ensure that I engage with my network and their content, drop them a direct message and tell them how much I appreciate them for supporting me and my content. After all, these connections are advertising my brand story and message to a captive audience who are ready to listen and then advocate for you too.

Brand experience

> *'Brand experience is the heartbeat of any memorable brand.'*

It's not just about what you offer; it's about how you make people feel every step of the way. Your brand experience is the sum of every interaction— every message, every product, every service—and how they align with the core essence of who you are. It's what turns passive consumers into passionate advocates.

Imagine your brand as a story. Every touchpoint is a chapter that invites people into your world. But more than that, it empowers them, transforms them, and elevates their journey.

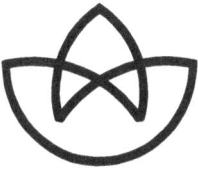

Brand experience is the heartbeat of any memorable brand.

——

VARSHA AMIN

Your audience doesn't just want to know what you stand for; they want to *feel* it in every interaction. That emotional connection becomes the foundation of trust and loyalty.

To build a brand that stands out in the crowd, focus on creating a holistic experience that resonates deeply. It's about consistency and authenticity—staying true to your values while delivering moments that surprise and delight. When you design a brand experience that is unforgettable, you give your audience more than a product; you give them a lasting impression that shapes how they see the world and, more importantly, how they see themselves.

In the end, the experience you craft isn't just about building a brand; it's about building a legacy. Be intentional, be powerful, and create something that others can't help but remember.

Who benefits?

In short, everyone.

Whether you're aspiring to work for MAANG (Meta, Amazon, Apple, Netflix or Google) or have other plans to invent something new, or you're a CMO at a tech company, a working parent striving to make an impact, or a young professional stiving to succeed in tech, building your personal brand will get you to places that you never imagined you could get to. And this is particularly true if you believe you're under-represented or believe you have been marginalised in any way, because you're a working mother, neurodiverse, you have an ethnic background, you come from the LGBTQ+ community, or basically because you're different (from the rest).

For CEOs and CMOs, personal branding is crucial in asserting their vision and influence, both within and outside their organisations. As individuals at the forefront of market trends and consumer behaviour, CEOs and CMOs can leverage personal branding to become thought leaders, influencing the direction of their industry and shaping the narrative around emerging technologies.

The broader picture

But this goes beyond just the individual benefits. It contributes to a larger world of ideas, innovations, and collaborative efforts. When diverse voices are heard and recognised, it fosters an environment of inclusivity and creativity, essential for the sustained growth and evolution of the tech industry.

Personal branding for under-represented people in the tech industry is both a pathway to personal recognition and success, and a catalyst for broader change, promoting diversity, inclusivity and innovation. It is a tool for these individuals to assert their presence, share their unique insights and, ultimately, drive meaningful change in an industry that is at the forefront of shaping our future. So, you're changing your own life for the better, and effecting change on the world around you!

Picture this: each chapter of my life—from humble '80s beginnings to corporate hurdles and my eventual renaissance—crafted my brand's DNA. But we're in an era where AI can compress years of brand-building into mere months, which is intriguing. In the not-so-distant past, elevating a personal brand to a point of recognition was a marathon, often spanning over a year. With the emergence of Generative AI technologies, like ChatGPT and Google's Gemini, you can envision rocketing from anonymity to a commanding online presence in just three months. How exhilarating is that? Let me share some technologies that can help to power your voice and your personal brand.

3. TOOLS TO BECOME AN AI-POWERED BRAND

'Master AI... before it masters you.'

There is a big possibility that Generative AI will trim down marketing teams, making them leaner, and even bring more competition to the table for your new business idea. So, it is important that you quickly upskill yourself on how to use GenAI. There's nothing to fear. If you have a fear, it is totally irrational, most likely fuelled by the media.

GenAI holds the potential to challenge stereotypes and biases. By enabling the creation of diverse and inclusive content, AI can play a really important role in reshaping the narratives around marginalised communities. This can involve generating images that represent diverse individuals in various roles, creating texts that challenge existing stereotypes, or producing audio content that represents a wider range of voices and accents. In doing so, AI can help in normalising diversity and inclusivity, thereby contributing to a more equitable digital landscape.

And that's not all. The integration of AI in content creation can also aid in enhancing the accessibility of digital platforms for the neurodiverse community. Tools that generate content that is more comprehensible and engaging for individuals with different cognitive abilities can make digital spaces more inclusive. This not only benefits the neurodiverse community by providing them with better access to information and resources but also enriches the digital ecosystem with their unique perspectives and contributions.

It is important, however, to acknowledge the ethical considerations and challenges that accompany the use of GenAI. Issues such as data privacy, the potential for perpetuating biases, and the implications of AI-generated content on employment in creative fields are critical to address. In fact, this field is in its infancy, so the coming years will be very interesting in terms of the direction this could go. In any case, ensuring that the deployment of AI is ethical, transparent and inclusive is paramount to harnessing its full potential for enhancing visibility for marginalised groups.

Therefore, the advent of GenAI presents an extraordinary opportunity for individuals and brands, especially for those from marginalised backgrounds. By facilitating easier access to content creation, enabling targeted outreach, challenging stereotypes, and enhancing digital accessibility, AI can be a game-changer when it comes to levelling the digital playing field. And yes, while we need to embrace these opportunities, we also need to remain vigilant about the ethical implications and strive towards an inclusive and equitable digital future.

So, what are the different tools that are available? There are a ton of them out there, but here are a few that you could use to speed up the process of getting your voice heard!

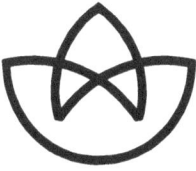

Master AI...before it masters you.

VARSHA AMIN

Text-based GenAI tools to amplify your brand's content

'Master AI, then use it to amplify your brand's visibility.'

AI tools are a great way to scale your brand fast, without investing in expensive content creators. Let's start with text-based ones and run through some of the tools that you can use to maximise your brand's AI amplification.

1. ChatGPT

The emergence of ChatGPT, a sophisticated language model developed by OpenAI, marked a significant milestone in the realm of digital content creation. This state-of-the-art tool has revolutionised the way written material is generated, offering a huge range of possibilities for creators across various domains, be it background, location, age, etcetera.

ChatGPT's impact is particularly profound in the generation of high quality written content, such as blog posts, social media updates and comprehensive articles. Its implications extend way beyond being a simple convenience, opening doors to a world where marginalised voices can find a more prominent platform to assist them in expressing their narratives and insights, thus enriching the digital landscape with a diverse range of perspectives.

At its core, ChatGPT is a flag-bearer to the advancements in the field of AI. It operates by understanding and generating human-like text, which enables it to assist in the creation of content that is both engaging and relevant—for the most part. Learning how to prompt it for the best output is key. This capability is genuinely transformative for content creators, including marketers, bloggers, educators, and activists, as it streamlines the process of ideation and writing. The model's ability to produce coherent, contextually appropriate, and stylistically varied text, makes it an invaluable tool for anyone looking to create written content.

If, like me, you're dyslexic, ChatGPT can enable you to get your message to your audience faster, since it has the ability to write content at lightning speed. Technology has always been an enabler for me; however, human creativity must come first to get the best output from technologies like ChatGPT. I mainly use it to structure and edit my content, but the planning, ideas and creativity sit with me. For example, I use it as my copyeditor. I ask it to check through my spelling and grammar. Or to rewrite an email that's too waffly. It helps me to get to the point. I have also asked it to be my executive coach, helping me to navigate through work, and even when I have been feeling overwhelmed.

When I was writing this book and emotions were running high, it responded to say:

> *'Remember, you've already come so far, and that alone shows your strength and determination. Writing a book is no small feat, especially with the challenges you've faced, but you're doing it. Focus on one step at a time, and trust in your voice—because your story and insights are valuable.*

Believe in the process and, most importantly, believe in yourself. Courage isn't about not feeling fear or doubt; it's about moving forward despite them. Take a deep breath and know that you have everything you need within you to finish this.

You're closer to the finish line than you think. Keep going!

2. Gemini by Google

Think of Gemini as a helpful friend who can assist you with various tasks, from writing emails and creating presentations to researching information and answering questions. It's designed to make your life easier and more efficient by providing information and completing tasks quickly and accurately.

OK, so you're a tech professional from an under-represented group. You want to share your experiences and insights to inspire others and to promote diversity in the industry. Gemini can be your digital ally.

For example, you want to write a blog post about overcoming challenges as a woman in tech. Gemini can help you to:

Research: *'Find me statistics about the gender gap in the tech industry.'*

Brainstorm ideas: *'Give me some personal anecdotes to share in my blog post.'*

Write drafts: *'Help me write a compelling introduction to my blog post.'*

Edit and proofread: *'Check my blog post for clarity and inclusivity.'*

Gemini can also suggest social media posts to share your blog post with a wider audience. This way, you can focus on sharing your story, and Gemini can handle the technical aspects of your online presence.

Remember, while these tools are useful, it's important to use these as a supplement to your own creativity and expertise. And always review and edit the content they generate to ensure it aligns with your personal brand, goals, and accurately reflects the facts.

It doesn't stop with text-based prompts. AI is also great at helping you with visual elements.

Let's now explore image-based tools.

Image and video-based GenAI tools to amplify your brand's content

1. Canva and Adobe AI

The integration of AI into graphic design platforms like Canva and Adobe represents yet another transformative leap in the field of digital asset creation. These advancements have not only simplified the design process but have also significantly enhanced the quality of outputs, making professional-grade graphic design more accessible to a broader range of users. This democratisation of design is, similarly to ChatGPT, particularly impactful for under-represented communities, offering them new avenues to craft and disseminate visual narratives that resonate deeply with their identities and messages—something that may previously have been an extreme challenge.

Canva and Adobe, both leaders in the digital and creative design space, have taken the leap and pioneered the integration of AI in their platforms, each offering unique capabilities that cater to a wide spectrum of design needs. Canva, known for its user-friendly interface (the saving grace of many a marketing department) has implemented AI to make design more intuitive and efficient. This includes features like automatic alignment and colour palette suggestions, which helps users create aesthetically pleasing designs without needing extensive design knowledge. Adobe, with its suite of professional design tools, employs AI to streamline complex tasks such as image editing, pattern generation and typography. These AI features are embedded in popular Adobe applications like Photoshop, Illustrator and Adobe XD, enhancing the capabilities of professional designers and novices alike.

Indeed, I have personally worked with professional graphic designers who've benefited from the time-saving benefits of these tools, which has been instrumental in increasing their well-being!

Adobe's AI feature has an 'object aware editing system' which helps users move and edit objects with ease. The new tool allows users to remove objects and people in an image or insert new objects in an image, like replacing a phone in someone's hand with a bouquet of flowers. It also allows users to change part of an image, like changing the colour or type of clothing a person is wearing in a photo.

Canva's Magic Media lets you generate images and videos from a simple text prompt in seconds. Type what you're looking for, choose your preferred style and size, and watch as it generates your image and videos for you. So, now you can get super creative with your visuals by creating striking images and videos that stand in line with your personal brand.

And once again, the significance of these AI-enhanced tools is particularly pronounced for under-represented communities. We live in a world where visual communication is paramount, so the ability to create compelling graphics is crucial for these groups to effectively convey their stories, culture and messages. Typically, the lack of access to expensive design software or professional design skills has been a barrier for these communities in asserting their presence in the digital and visual world.

2. Midjourney

Midjourney is a powerful AI tool that specialises in generating images from text descriptions. It can create stunning visuals in various styles, from realistic to abstract, based on your prompts.

Here is a brief overview of its capabilities:

Image Generation: *You can provide a text description, and Midjourney will create an image that matches your vision.*

Style Control: *You can specify the desired style, such as anime, oil painting or watercolour, to influence the output.*

Image Editing: *Midjourney can also be used to edit and enhance existing images.*

High-Quality Output: *The tool produces high-resolution images that are often indistinguishable from human-created artwork.*

Midjourney is a valuable tool for artists and designers, or anyone who needs to create visually compelling content. If you fancy getting creative with your brand, then it's worth exploring this.

3. **Runway**

The realm of movie creation and video content production has also been significantly transformed by the advent of AI tools such as Runway. These AI-powered platforms offer ground-breaking capabilities that are reshaping the landscape of film-making, particularly for independent and marginalised creators who often face barriers in accessing traditional film-making resources.

Runway stands out in the field of AI-driven content creation due to its advanced features and user-friendly interfaces. It harnesses the power of AI to simplify complex video editing and production processes, enabling users to create high quality movies and video content with considerably less resource investment than traditional methods.

Runway offers a suite of AI tools tailored for video editing and production. It includes features like automatic object removal, motion tracking, and smart background replacement. These functionalities allow creators to achieve visual effects that would typically require extensive post-production work and sophisticated software. For independent film-makers and content creators, this means being able to execute creative visions that were previously out of reach due to budget constraints or lack of technical expertise.

The impact of these AI tools is perhaps the most profound of all, especially for marginalised creators. Traditionally, film production has been an expensive endeavour, often requiring substantial financial investment in equipment, software, and skilled personnel. This has posed a significant barrier for creators from under-represented communities, who may lack the financial means or access to industry networks. With Runway, these creators can now produce high quality content that competes with traditionally produced films.

These tools, like the others, democratise the creative process, allowing film-makers to experiment with different styles and techniques that would otherwise be constrained by budget and resource limitations. This fosters innovation and diversity in film and video content, as creators from various backgrounds can bring their unique perspectives and storytelling approaches to the forefront.

In addition to facilitating the creative process, AI-driven tools like Runway also streamline production workflows. Tasks that would typically take hours or days to complete can now be accomplished in a fraction of the time. This efficiency not only reduces production costs but also enables creators to focus more on the creative aspects of film-making rather than being hindered by technical nightmares.

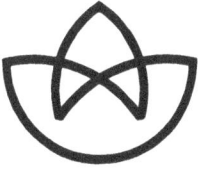

Master AI, then use it to amplify your brand's visibility.

———
VARSHA AMIN

4. TURN YOUR IDEA INTO MONEY

OK, so we've covered the different types of AI tool that can help you to create content for your personal brand. But how can AI help your business to make money?

Business transactions are a bit of a dry topic, but some of the AI developments have added a bit of flavour. Financial tools powered by AI, such as Square (I personally use Square and love them), have emerged as game-changers, particularly for small businesses and independent creators. These tools are about facilitating transactions of course, but they are reshaping the way that entrepreneurs manage their finances, with a significant positive impact on marginalised business owners who often face challenges in accessing and navigating traditional financial systems.

Invoicing tools like Square

Square, known for its innovative approach to financial services, is taking the lead on how AI can be leveraged to streamline business operations. At its core, Square provides an efficient invoicing solution, simplifying a process that is fundamental yet often cumbersome for small business owners.

You can now even use Square to take payments for physical and non-physical goods over the Square app. I mean, this is brilliant—no extra kit to buy. It's liberating for a tiny business that wants to make goods accessible to under-represented communities and marginalised groups, because you can now access people everywhere and you no longer need a store. You just need micro communities of people to spread the word and mobilise people that have dreams of making profit with purpose.

In summary

So, all in all, AI offers a suite of tools that not only democratise content creation but also provide a platform for amplifying diverse voices. By leveraging these technologies, marginalised groups can gain more visibility and contribute significantly to the digital narrative. This promotes inclusivity and diversity in the digital realm, ensuring that the digital landscape is a true reflection of the diverse society in which we live.

Hopefully, you can see how AI forms a huge part of the potential growth of your personal brand. Some of us—me included—are from marginalised backgrounds. How many times did you see the words 'marginalised background' throughout the AI discussion, prominently placed next to some kind of benefit? That in itself is a giant leap forward. Dry technological discussion aside, I truly feel that AI may someday come to be known as 'the great leveller', because the possibilities for improving the lives of marginalised people are endless.

But it's not always rosy.

5. THE PROBLEM WITH UNREGULATED AI

There are some concerns—like with any new technology—and the use of AI raises important questions. It is crucial to find a balance where AI complements human creativity and skill, rather than replacing it. Additionally, ensuring ethical use of AI in content creation, especially regarding copyright and representation, is very important, particularly if you don't want to end up in a sea of litigation. Here are some important limitations to consider:

AI limitations:

- AI cannot learn independently; it relies on human-provided data, which can lead to bias if the data is flawed.

- AI can produce incorrect outputs—called hallucinations—which is why human evaluation is so critical. If the AI is used solely to make decisions on our behalf, we're in big trouble of jeopardising marginalised and under-represented groups!

- AI tools can also be affected by systemic bias which exist in healthcare, education, or in legal systems, that could place marginalised groups at a big disadvantage, if it's not governed effectively.

- When AI tools are trained on biased data, they can reinforce stereotypes and exclude under-represented groups. This means people from diverse backgrounds may be misrepresented or left out entirely, making it harder for them to succeed or to be seen. To truly change the narrative, we must challenge these biases.

Always check with a human:

- Human input is crucial to ensure AI outputs are accurate, ethical, and aligned with your brand values.

- Trust human intelligence over artificial intelligence to ensure a people-first approach. AI is there to be leveraged, but don't make the mistake of outsourcing everything. You'll be surprised at what some organisations and individuals do in the pursuit of adopting an all-AI approach. We must remind ourselves who we are serving—is it AI or humans?

- Collaboration between technical roles and non-technical roles is a must-have in order to use AI responsibly and for effective implementation in workplaces and at home.

6. BRAND AMPLIFICATION AND AI

'If you amplify your brand, your brand will amplify you.'

Platforms are a great way to amplify your brand, and they can come in many guises. It could be communities that you are a part of and leverage, or individual influencers. And these could be micro or nano influencers that could have larger communities or networks than yours. Let's explore these a little more.

Platforms give you wider reach which scales your brand's voice

Don't get caught up in vanity metrics, as tempting as it can be. The influencer who has a million followers will likely miss you in a pool of thousands of conversations. But engaging with other reputable community members will give you a stepping stone. For example, the thought-leader that you're trying to connect with and who is perhaps too busy, might be somebody that you'll never catch even when you're chasing. Instead, start engaging with those that are less known and who are accessible. This way, you start building an emotional connection with those people who believe in what you believe. You can call it relationship building but be sure to build for a long-term relationship or partnership.

Many people view brand as a short-term approach, but the most effective way to brand is to have consistency and an always-on approach. Brand campaigns should be run like evergreen content campaigns. A one-hit wonder will give you fame, but it won't build your brand equity. This is how you start to brand organically. A platform is there to amplify your brand voice and message, so be sure to use it wisely.

If a community is asking for a membership fee, firstly work out if you can afford it, and then see if there may be a sizeable return. If there isn't, then join those that are low risk. For example, one community that I've recently come across is pitched at the premium market and one year's membership is $3600 which breaks down at $300 a month— an insane sum of money. But if it means in the long-term that your salary as a business owner, employee, or a personal brand, increases by $20k, then it's money well spent, particularly with the connections that you make. After all, you can't put a price on relationships.

After reading Ted Rubin's book *Return on Relationship*, I have truly come to understand that relationships are the new currency in today's digital economy. Ted Rubin, who I met in person back in 2014, keeps in touch by wishing me happy birthday every year on Facebook, without fail. Now that's a personal brand that I admire and like associating with, because he keeps his word without fail.

Becoming a thought leader, to establish yourself as an expert in your field

This could involve writing articles, contributing to industry publications, or regularly posting insightful content on social media. As a thought leader, you can influence others, shape industry conversations, and increase your professional value.

- Write that blog

- Write that social post

- Write that book you've been dreaming of for over a decade

- Join communities or consider contributing to articles

Here's the thing—if you're struggling to start, feel free to start using AI as a launchpad. It still takes me a while to fine-tune what Sai outputs, but it's a great starting point for someone like me who has little time to think, let alone write.

Collaboration with micro-influencers and content creators

Partner with micro-influencers and content creators who align with your brand values. They can help amplify your message to a wider audience. These collaborations can take various forms, such as guest blogging, social media takeovers, or co-hosting events. The LinkedIn community is a great place to start. This is because there is a real sense of community, although don't get me wrong, you do still get trolls.

LinkedIn's platform, owned by Microsoft, is empowering for those that don't have a voice— its algorithms favour the under-represented—whereas meta-based networks I have found can favour big influencers.

Partnerships with organisations

Partner with larger organisations to scale your reach. By piggybacking on their marketing efforts, you can gain access to a broader audience. These partnerships can be mutually beneficial and can include joint ventures, sponsorships, or affiliate marketing.

When I started building my business and brand, I spoke for free (or for a nominal fee) everywhere in Winchester between 2018–2020, but things truly changed when I landed back in London. There is so much that the average person may say against the Capital, but London loved me back. I'm so grateful.

I landed a partnership with a big tech giant, where I was able to deliver my personal branding know-how to groups of diverse people from under-represented backgrounds in tech. The tech giant that I'm describing is a forward-thinking, innovative and creative brand—a brand that is designed for the creator economy. Working with this tech brand has been so much fun, because their values align with my brand values, and my primary archetype is The Creator, and so is theirs. Like attracts like, so it's important you know what you're like. You'd be surprised at the number of clients and people I talk to who don't actually know what they are like. You get the picture.

Other organisations and not-for-profit companies

The #ChangeTheFace initiative aligns perfectly with my mission to empower those people who feel marginalised and under-represented in tech. It's a movement calling for change, urging the industry to better reflect the diversity of the world we live in. For too long, the tech industry has been dominated by a narrow demographic, leaving many feeling as though they don't belong.

If you amplify your brand, your brand will amplify you.

— VARSHA AMIN

7. CHALLENGES TO BUILDING A PERSONAL BRAND

Building a personal brand is one of the most rewarding journeys that you can embark upon, but it's not without its challenges. Along the way, you'll encounter obstacles that test your resilience, confidence, and mental strength. However, these challenges are not roadblocks; they are opportunities to grow. Each difficulty that you face is an opportunity to refine your approach, strengthen your resolve, and build a brand that reflects the best version of you.

Let's explore some of the most common challenges, and how to overcome them.

Lack of confidence

Self-doubt can paralyse even the most talented individuals. You may question your abilities, wondering if you're truly capable of building a brand that stands out. The key to overcoming this is cultivating self-belief. Start with affirmations—simple yet powerful statements that reaffirm your strengths and potential. Consistently remind yourself that you are enough, that your voice matters, and that you are capable of creating a brand that represents your unique brilliance. Confidence isn't a trait; it's a practice. Work on it daily.

Fear of failure and irrelevance

Fear can be crippling, especially when you think about failing or being overlooked. But here's the truth: if you fail, most people won't notice. And if they do, they'll forget about it quickly. The solution lies in perseverance. Failure isn't final—it's feedback. Adjust your strategy, optimise your techniques, and keep moving toward your goals. Remember, the only way to become irrelevant is to give up. As long as you're willing to evolve, your brand will continue to grow.

Isolation and loneliness

Building a brand, especially when you're running a business on your own, can be incredibly isolating. It's easy to feel disconnected from others when all the responsibility rests on your shoulders. This is why self-worth, self-care and self-love become essential tools. You must prioritise your mental and emotional wellbeing to avoid burnout. Surround yourself with a supportive community, even if it's virtual. Lean on others for encouragement and remind yourself that you're not alone in this journey.

Burnout and mental health

Entrepreneurial burnout is real. The anxiety of always being 'on', coupled with thoughts of giving up, can take a toll on your mental health. Social media can be a double-edged sword—offering purpose and connection but also pulling you into the toxic comparison trap. You might start measuring your worth by likes and comments, which can drain your self-esteem. To overcome this, disconnect from the noise and reconnect with your 'why'. Focus on your mission, not the metrics. Take breaks when needed and remember that your mental health is non-negotiable.

Lack of time

For driven individuals, time feels like an elusive resource. There never seem to be enough hours in the day, especially in a fast-paced, always-on world. The key here is prioritisation. Focus on what truly matters. Delegate where possible, automate tasks with technology, and protect your time by setting boundaries. It's not about doing everything— it's about doing the right things that move your brand forward.

Lack of tools, resources and knowledge

You won't have all the tools or knowledge right away, and that's okay. What's important is your willingness to learn and adapt. Start by picking one tool, one resource, or one area of knowledge to focus on each month. Master it, then move to the next. In 90 days, you'll be more efficient, more informed, and significantly more confident. With confidence comes power, and that power will fuel your brand's success.

The naysayers

Along the way, you'll encounter people who doubt your vision. They'll say it's never been done, so you won't succeed. But that's because they don't see what you see. Don't let their opinions overshadow your inner voice. Stay true to your unique perspective, and let others inspire you without copying them. Authenticity is your greatest asset. It's what will set you apart and sustain your brand in the long run. Trust me, staying true to yourself will lead to lasting success.

Find your happiness and serve others

Building a brand isn't just about reaching goals; it's about finding joy in the process. Find your happiness, focus on serving others, and success will follow. When your work is aligned with your passion and purpose, your brand becomes a force of impact—not just for yourself, but for everyone you touch. Keep going, stay true to your path, and let your brand shine.

Lessons learnt

I believe that I'm successful today because I believe in the power of my own kindness—like attracts like. You can be kind, but assertive and firm—but remember to speak up if there's something that you don't agree with. The worst-case scenario is to agree to disagree, right? You have nothing to lose. Don't stop being kind just because you see successful people that aren't. Their success will not last. People won't remember your title—they'll remember how you made them feel.

The people who care will always be there for you, at your highest point, but also at your lowest point. They'll be your ultimate cheerleaders.

GenAI has been an enabler for me. It has helped by providing tools that compensated for my dyslexia and allowed me to focus on my strengths. It has showed me that technology can be an ally in addressing personal and professional challenges.

Personal branding for me has always been about daring to be different. For members of the LGBTQ+ community, people of colour, and the neurodiverse, being different is not a choice but a reality. We often face unique challenges in being seen and heard. However, by embracing our differences and using them to shape our personal brand, we can make our voices heard. It's about turning our unique experiences into a narrative that resonates with others and inspires change.

Through my personal branding journey, I've learned the importance of being authentic and transparent. It's about letting the world see the real you, with all your imperfections and strengths. This authenticity not only builds trust but also creates a deeper connection with your audience.

In overcoming these obstacles, I realised that personal branding is more than a career tool; it's a form of self-expression and empowerment. It's about taking control of your narrative and using your unique voice to make an impact. Whether it's through speaking engagements, social media, or mentoring, every action that I take is an opportunity to reinforce my brand and what I stand for.

To those facing similar challenges, my advice is to embrace your story. Use your personal brand to showcase not just your achievements, but your journey, including the obstacles you have overcome. Remember, it's our unique experiences and perspectives that make us stand out. In the tech industry and beyond, there's a need for diverse voices and stories. By daring to be different and using personal branding as a tool, we can not only overcome our challenges but also pave the way for a more inclusive and diverse professional world.

Summary

We've looked at my unique journey and how it informed and evolved who I am as a person, and how my brand now stands as a unique and almost sentient form. The same goes for you—your most potent tool in the realm of personal branding is your unique life narrative. My journey from the '80s to my rebirth in 2018 (and beyond) has sculpted my Brand DNA, and similarly your life's saga will shape your brand's essence. Your story, with its rollercoaster of highs and lows, is the blueprint of your brand.

8. WHAT NEXT?

You'll know from my story that in my formative years, being different felt like a curse. Whether navigating the cultural maze as a child of immigrants or feeling like an academic misfit, my uniqueness felt like a burden. Over time I have realised it's my unique lens that offers me a fresh approach to problem-solving and innovation. Each challenge you've conquered adds a layer of depth to your brand, making it relatable and human. Your struggles and triumphs aren't just life events; they're your badges of resilience and fortitude. They're what make you, well, you.

You've been through my journey, and hopefully you've been pondering on your own. Through this enriching experience, you should be able to see that one axiom remains constant: your personal brand and Brand DNA are not separate entities but intertwined extensions of you. They manifest in every dialogue, every choice and every endeavour you undertake. Their symbiosis is akin to a dance—a dance that enriches both.

A manifesto for the trailblazers of tomorrow

So, what does this look like for you? Understanding the architecture of your brand is crucial, but let's not forget it is action that turns the wheel of transformation. You've got the tools, the know-how, and the vision to breathe life into your personal brand and Brand DNA. So, what's next? Whether it's revising your mission statement, rebranding your visual identity, or networking with a purpose, each meticulous step that you take is where your brand leaps from paper to reality.

You've taken the first step with me—you've read my story and understood how it impacted my personal growth. You've seen how that journey evolved my personal brand and how that DNA became—and maybe always was—synonymous with me as a unique human being.

There's no time for excuses, and I dare say you aren't the type to make them. We get one chance to make this work, one chance to leave our mark on the people around us and the wider world. How will you be remembered? As someone who hesitated, who hid away, who was ashamed of who they are? Or as someone who was brave, and faced it all, and helped others when they could? Someone who was truthful and dependable and inspiring? Is that you? I believe it is. And I believe that of myself. It's what I strive to be, and sometimes am, and I'll never stop striving for that. After all, if I were to allow myself to slip down into a lesser version of myself, I'd be unable to impart an example in my vocation of motherhood. Of course, it's not just mothers who need to be able to impart this sort of inspiration and example, but this is fundamental and personal to me, as well as another example of objective authenticity. I think you are like me, in terms of dreaming of a better world, and dreaming of a world where you can share who you really are loud and clear.

So, here's to you—the dreamer, the maverick, the changemaker. A toast to your personal brand and your extraordinary Brand DNA; an ovation for the incredible sojourn that beckons, a journey sculpted by your uniqueness.

Embrace your essence.
Dare to be different.
Liberate your potential.
Reshape the world.
Your brand, in your hands—it starts with YOU.
I look forward to changing the world with YOU.

JOIN THE 'DIFFERENT' COMMUNITY

Together we can build a better world for our children and for future generations to come.

Just as the lotus flower rises from the mud, blooming with resilience and beauty, for under-represented communities in tech, this symbolises our collective strength and growth, even in challenging environments.

Together, we can break through barriers, lifting each other up to become a powerful force for good. Like the lotus, we flourish, proving that from adversity, greatness can emerge. Let's grow and transform the tech world, one step at a time.

A kinder world is an inclusive world for all.

Steps to being a part of the Different Community are:

1.   Follow me and connect on LinkedIn: www.linkedin.com/in/varsha-amin

2.   Join the Different Community here: https://www.linkedin.com/company/varsha-amin-different/

Together, we can elevate each other, be seen and heard.

I look forward to seeing you there!

ACKNOWLEDGEMENTS

This book is the result of my own experience, as well as countless voices, stories, and moments that have shaped its pages. To everyone who supported me on this journey— thank you.

First and foremost, I want to express my gratitude to my husband, Jay, and to our two beautiful girls, Arya and Ava, whose unwavering belief in me gave me the strength to keep going. Your love and encouragement have been my guiding light.

To the phenomenal Francis Murphy who helped me craft and shape this book.

To my talented designer, Jonny Tavener, who produced the design assets of this book.

To my amazing community of well-wishers; including Faith Ruto, who has been my champion throughout.

To the incredible individuals who shared their stories for this book: thank you for your honesty, vulnerability, and trust. Your experiences are the heart of this work, and your courage will inspire others for years to come.

ACKNOWLEDGEMENTS

To my readers—whether you're picking up this book to learn, grow, or simply feel seen and heard—this is for you. Your curiosity and courage are the reasons I wrote this.

To my critics: thank you for your doubts and challenges. You pushed me to dig deeper, work harder, and prove to myself that I could do this. Your scepticism became my motivation.

Lastly, I want to acknowledge everyone working to amplify the voices of under-represented communities in tech. Together, we are building a future that values difference and celebrates authenticity.

I thank you all—from the bottom of my heart.

ABOUT THE AUTHOR

Varsha Amin is an award-winning brand marketer and strategist with a passion for empowering individuals and businesses to thrive through the power of their brand. With years of experience working with UK and global clients, Varsha specialises in leveraging AI and technology to build and scale impactful personal and business brands.

In 2019, Varsha served as a trainer for Facebook's Digital Skills Programme, equipping leaders and students with cutting-edge skills in innovation, technology and AI. Her expertise has supported leading brands such as Apple, Adobe, Microsoft, Vodafone, O2, Builder.ai, and lastminute. com.

Through her work, Varsha has trained over 500 professionals, including students, working parents, entrepreneurs, and corporate leaders, helping them unlock their potential and navigate the fast-paced tech landscape.

In 2020, BBC tech news featured Varsha in celebration of Ada Lovelace Day, highlighting her resilience in adapting to the pandemic and advocating for digital skills in STEM.

Varsha's mission is clear: to inspire, empower, and elevate under-represented voices in tech and beyond, ensuring they find their place and leave their mark in an ever-evolving AI and digital world.

Connect with Varsha:

LinkedIn: www.linkedin.com/in/varsha-amin

Instagram: @varsha.amin

Websites:

www.varshaamin.com

www.lotusx.co.uk